Robinson Crusoe

A Pantomime by
John Crocker

Lyrics and Music by
Eric Gilder

Evans Plays London

ISBN 0 237 74975 0

Printed in Great Britain by Lewis Reprints Ltd., member of Brown Knight & Truscott Group, London and Tonbridge

PRODUCTION NOTE

Pantomime, as we know it today, is a form of entertainment all on its own, derived from a number of different sources - the commedia dell'arte (and all that that derived from), the ballet, opera, music hall and the realms of folk-lore and fairy tale. And elements of all of these are still to be found in it. This strange mixture has created a splendid topsy-turvy world where men are women, women are men, where the present is embraced within the past, where people are hit but not hurt, where authority is constantly flouted, where everything is open to ridicule including pantomime itself at times and, above all, where magic abounds and dreams invariably come true. In other words, it is - or should be - fun. Fun to do and fun to watch and the sense of enjoyment which can be conveyed by a cast is very important to the enjoyment of the audience.

Pantomime can be very simply staged if resources are limited. Basically a tab surround at the back, tab legs at the sides and a set of traverse tabs for the frontcloth scenes, together with the simplest of cut-out pieces to suggest the various locales, (or even just placards with this information written on them), will suffice. Conversely, there is no limit to the extent to which more lavish facilities can be employed.

The directions I have given in the text adopt a middle course and are based on a permanent setting of a cyclorama sky-cloth at the back, a few feet in front of which is a rostrum about two feet high running the width of the stage. About two-thirds of the depth downstage is a false proscenium, immediately behind which are the lines for a set of traverse tabs. Below the false proscenium are arched entrances left and right with reveals if necessary to the proscenium. A border will be required at some point between the false proscenium and the cyclorama to mask lighting battens and the top of the cyclorama. Lastly, there are sets of steps leading down into the auditorium at both the front corners of the stage.

Into this permanent setting are placed cut-out backings and various wings left and right. The frontcloth fly lines come in behind the traverse tabs. Cloths can, of course, be tumbled or rolled if flying space is limited. I have indicated that the traverse tabs should be closed for the beginning of most frontcloth scenes, then if any hitch occurs while flying in the cloth the lights can still come up and the actors get on with the scene. Similarly I have, where possible, given cues before the ends of these scenes for the tabs to be closed again to allow time for cloths to be flown out. Thus, each scene can flow swiftly into the next, an important point if a smooth-running production is to be achieved.

The settings and costumes should preferably be in clear bright colours to give a story book effect. I think it best to have everything in one period, apart from deliberate anachronisms in some of the comics' costumes. In Defoe's story Crusoe was shipwrecked in 1659 and this period, which is virtually Restoration, is, of course, highly suitable. Scene 4 is mainly a U.V. sequence so the principals appearing in it will need costumes made of fluorescent material, which is obtainable in a wide variety of colours from Barnums Carnival Novelties, 67 Hammersmith Road, W.14., and other theatrical suppliers. Such costumes can be worn in other scenes with ordinary lighting; indeed, it is desirable for identification purposes that they should be worn at least in the previous scene. It will also be necessary for each character to wear some form of headgear, otherwise in the U.V. light they will appear to be headless!

The U.V. equipment needed can be hired from the usual stage electrical suppliers as can a cloud projector if it is used for Scene 3, a ripple projector for Scenes 4 and 5 and a Freeze light for the running sequence at the end of Scene 9, also the maroons in Scene 10 and flash boxes and powder for the flashes throughout. As for the rest of the lighting I have not attempted to give a lighting plot as this entirely depends on the equipment available, but generally speaking most pantomime lighting should be full up, warm and bright. Pinks and ambers are probably best for this and a circuit of blues in the cyclorama battens would be useful for the dawn rise and dramatic effects in general. Follow spots are a great help, but not essential. If they are available it is often effective in romantic numbers to fade out the stage lighting and hold the principals in the follow spots, quickly fading up the full lighting on the last few bars because this can help to increase the applause!

Pantomime needs many props and often they will have to be home-made. Instructions are given in the prop plot for any of the more awkward seeming ones. Props should also be colourfully painted and in pantomime most of them should be larger than reality. It is also wise for the property master to examine carefully the practical use to which a prop is to be put; often a whole comedy sequence depends on something working properly. The guns in Scenes 6 and 10 need not be practical. A starting pistol used offstage is quite sufficient for the gunshots and I have therefore marked them as effects.

The music has been specially composed so that it is easy for the less musically accomplished to master, but it is also scored in parts for the more musically ambitious. If an orchestra is available well and good, but a single piano will suffice. It is an advantage, however, if there can be a drummer as well; not only because a rhythm accompaniment enhances the numbers, but also because, for some reason never yet fully fathomed, slapstick hits and falls seem twice as funny if they coincide with a well-timed bonk on a drum, wood-block or whatever is found to make the noise best suited to the action.

Pantomime demands a particular style of playing and production. The acting must be larger than life, but still sincere, with a good deal of sparkle and attack. Much of it must be projected directly at the audience, since one of pantomime's great advantages is that it deliberately breaks down the "fourth wall". The actors can literally and metaphorically shake hands with their audience who become almost members of the cast; indeed, their active participation from time to time is essential. A word of warning on this, though - the actors must always remain in control; they must never encourage a response to such an extent that they can no longer be heard. This is particularly so in the case of hissing, which I think Davy Jones and Will Atkins should discourage. If their every appearance is drowned in a sea of hisses much of the effect of their parts, and much of the plot too, will be lost. And the plot of a pantomime is of prime importance because the larger part of the audience, the children, like stories and like to be able to follow them. Therefore, the producer should ensure that the story line is always clearly brought out and treated with respect. An emphasis on teamwork will be a help here; every member of the cast should allow whoever has the important bit in a scene to be the focus of attention. The selfish actor continually hogging the limelight is distracting to the audience and very aggravating to the rest of the cast! There is always room for local gags and topical quips in pantomime, but they should not be overdone. Nor should any of the comedy - too much "milking" or too long dwelling on something which the cast think is hilarious but obviously the audience do not can slow down the pace disastrously, and much of this script should go at a pretty spanking pace. It should also be appreciated that any comedy scene needs rhythm and a shape; a big laugh in the wrong place can upset the balance and actually make the sequence as a whole less funny. Last, but certainly not least, the comedy must never appear to be conscious of its own funniness.

Characterization should be clear and definite. I prefer the traditional use of a man to play the Dame and a girl to play the Principal Boy. In the case of the Dame, anyway, there is a sound argument for this; audiences will laugh more readily at a man impersonating a woman involved in the mock cruelties of slapstick than at a real woman. For this reason an actor playing a Dame should never quite let us forget he is a man, while giving a sincere character performance of a woman; further, he can be as feminine as he likes but never effeminate. Mrs Crusoe is a lively lady, rumbustious even, and very much a "mum"

Like the Dame a Principal Boy also requires a character performance, but with the implications reversed, of course! An occasional slap of the thigh is not enough. Robinson is adventurous and enjoys any challenge which comes his way. He should also be allowed to have a sense of humour.

Principal Girls can be a bore, but only if they are presented as mere pretty symbols of feminine sweetness. Polly should indeed be pretty, but as she explains herself, she also has brains and determination and she too is not lacking in humour. Her sister, Sukey, is less shrewd, but more cute and impetuous.

Billy Crusoe is a successful failure. Things seldom turn out as he intends but this never disconcerts him for long. The actor playing him should to an extent exploit his own personality.

Will Atkins's villainy springs entirely from his love for Mrs Crusoe. We should feel his intentions to be diabolically sincere, their accomplishment is marred only by his hypochondria and his choice of associates. These, Jolly Roger and Rueful Rupert, are just as their names suggest. Roger is a convinced optimist, however wrong anything goes he will immediately convince himself it is right. Rupert is the exact opposite, stoic in his pessimism, but never miserable or bad-tempered.

Broody is all parrot - beadily suspicious, mischievous, cantankerous and yet affectionate, all at the same time.

Man Friday is a cheerful opportunist, never at a loss as to how to exploit any situation in which he finds himself. To do this he is well equipped since he has brains, ability and charm.

Britannia should be an imposing lady of commanding personality and presence. Though she should be played for comedy, it must be done sincerely and without burlesque. Her opponent, Davy Jones, is a jovial and disreputable old sea dog.

I have made provision for a Chorus of ten, but naturally the number used will depend on how many are available.

JOHN CROCKER

CHARACTERS

BILLY CRUSOE	
SUKEY PERKINS	
POLLY PERKINS	
MRS CRUSOE	
THE FAIRY BRITANNIA	
DAVY JONES	
ROBINSON CRUSOE	
BROODY	A parrot
WILL ATKINS	
JOLLY ROGER)	Hire Service Pirates
RUEFUL RUPERT)	
MAN FRIDAY	

CHORUS as Citizens, Sailors, Fishes, Davy Jones's Sea Guards, Sirens, Cannibals, Pirates and Serving Wenches.

SYNOPSIS OF SCENES

PART I

Scene 1.	The Port of Hull
Scene 2.	'Tween Decks on "The Venturer"
Scene 3.	The Main Deck
Scene 4.	All Adrift
Scene 5.	Davy Jones's Locker and transformation to Crusoe's Island

PART II

Scene 6.	Robinson Crusoe's Island
Scene 7.	Meanwhile, in Port of Spain
Scene 8.	The "Pieces of Eight" Tavern
Scene 9.	A Sleepy Lagoon
Scene 10.	The Stockade
Scene 11.	Pax Britannica
Scene 12.	The Wedding Feast aboard the Good Ship "Hopeful"

ROBINSON CRUSOE

MUSIC 1.   OVERTURE

PART I

Scene 1   The Port of Hull

Fullset. A flower-pot is set throughout in front of the false pros., L. The rostrum represents a raised quay. A cut-out of a low wall is set half-way back on the rostrum, running the length of it; behind this wall on the L. is the cut-out stern of a 17th century sailing ship with her name, "THE VENTURER", clearly showing. It is set on a narrow movable truck. The ship is tied up to a bollard D.S. of the wall. Stone steps lead down from the rostrum in C. There are two wings L. The upper one has a practical door over which is a sign - "PERKINS & PERKINS, MERCHANT VENTURERS, KINGSTON-UPON-HULL & PADDINGTON GREEN, LONDON". The lower wing is an Inn, "THE BULKHEAD AND BILGEPIPE", which also has a practical door. There is a water butt, with a lid on it, set at the onstage end of the Inn. (If there is not sufficient depth for two wings, hang the Inn sign over the exit below the false pros. and place the water butt beside the false pros.) On the R. is a house-piece in a decorative state of decay. Its D.S. end holds a door on which is a knocker and a doorknob; L. of the door is an old-fashioned bellpull; over the door is a porch canopy and above that a nameplate, "MON SEAVIEW REPOS". R. of the door is a painted window with a "VACANCIES" sign in it, wooden shutters on either side, a sill with flower-pots on it below and a sign with five stars and "BOARDING HOUSE. Prop., MRS CRUSOE" on it above. The U.S. end of the house shows the roof sloping down and has a chimney pot on it.

The CHORUS, as sailors and citizens are discovered.

MUSIC 2. "HEAVE HO!"

CHORUS

Heave ho! Give us a ship!
We're a seafarin' community.
We just long for a trip,
'Cos when we're ashore we are all at sea.
Our "Venturer" is at the quay-side,
Stuck in dock beside the seaside.
On her deck we long to reside
From this very day!
We all feel that we oughter
Live our lives on the water.
Cut the talk and let's get under way.

(Dance.)

All we need is a Banker!
Then we'll yank up the anchor,
Slip the hawser and out to sea
With nautical phraseology,
So cut the talk and let's get under way.

1st CHORUS But when is "The Venturer" going to sail?

2nd CHORUS Let's ask Billy Crusoe.

CHORUS Good idea. Billy! Billy Crusoe! etc.

(One of them knocks at the door of "PERKINS & PERKINS".)

BILLY (off L.) Coming! Coming!

(MUSIC 3. BILLY runs on from the office carrying a large pile of ledgers.)

What is it? I'm very busy balancing the books. (He trips and drops them.) I've failed. Anybody got a saucepan?

3rd CHORUS What for?

BILLY To cook the books. It's the only way I'll get them ready in time for Perkins and Perkins. They're coming here today. Both of them.

4th CHORUS What, the ship's owners?

5th CHORUS Ah, that sounds hopeful.

BILLY Oh, I don't know. They've never been here before, but they're probably only a couple of old gents.

5th CHORUS Yes, but why are they coming?

BILLY Merchant venturing, of course. With "The Venturer".

CHORUS Hurray!

6th CHORUS Who's going to be the Captain?

BILLY Ah. I was hoping they might choose me -

(CHORUS laugh.)

Well, I thought I could start at the top and work my way down. On the other hand they might choose my brother, Robinson.

CHORUS Robinson!

7th CHORUS But wasn't he taken prisoner by a Turkish pirate?

BILLY Yes, but he escaped and he should be back today.

(CHORUS give cries of astonishment and delight.)

Anyway, if you want to get taken on "The Venturer's" owners will be picking a crew at noon.

(CHORUS disperse chattering excitedly.)

I wish I could go to sea, though. I'm a rotten clerk. (He gathers up the ledgers.)

(MUSIC 4. SUKEY enters U.L., on rostrum, looking at a piece of paper in her hand.)

SUKEY Now along here and turn left, (She comes down steps.) and The Bulkhead and Bilgepipe should be just - (She bumps into BILLY knocking the ledgers over.)

BILLY Oh, really! (Indignantly.) Now look here – (He sees SUKEY.) No, don't look here. I'll look there.

SUKEY I say, I'm awfully sorry. Let me help you pick them up.

BILLY No, no, I couldn't think of it.

SUKEY Oh. Well then, I'll go and find the –

BILLY Wait! Maybe I could think of it after all.

(Both bend down.)

Which one would you like to pick up?

SUKEY How about this one?

BILLY (snatching it from her and throwing it aside) Oh no – far too heavy for you. (He picks up a slimmer one.) Try this one – much better quality paper, too. Feel it. (Rips out a sheet and gives it to her.)

SUKEY Oh, should you do that?

BILLY Why not? Plenty more here. In fact it's nothing but paper from beginning to end. Very dull reading though, just a lot of accounts.

SUKEY Really? You must be very rich then.

BILLY Oh no, very poor. I'm a clerk, you see. I'd much rather be a sailor, though – like my brother Robinson. My name's William, by the way, but everybody calls me Billy.

SUKEY And my name's Susan, but nobody uses that either. They call me Sue for short or Sukey for just as long.

BILLY Just as long as what?

SUKEY Just as long as you want to, I suppose.

BILLY Well, how long are you going to be here?

SUKEY I don't know. You see, I've just arrived from London with my sister Polly. I'm supposed to be looking for somewhere called The Bulkhead and Bilgepipe for us to stay.

BILLY What? You don't want to stay there. You want to stay in a good place. Like here. (Points at house R.) My mother runs it. Genuine five star accommodation.

(A star falls off board.)

Er four star.

(Another star falls.)

Three.

(And another.)

Two.

(Another.)

One.

(Last star slips but doesn't fall completely. SUKEY puts her hands over her ears then looks up.)

SUKEY I thought it was going to blast off.

BILLY Oh no. Very strongly built. I'll just get mother. Yes, it's solid as a rock. (Raises knocker to knock. It comes off in his hand. He laughs it off.) These modern screws. (Pulls on bell pull at side of door and goes on pulling so that a long length of wire comes out. EFFECT 1. Jingle of housebell off R.) Gives a very long ring, you see. (He throws bell pull and wire off D.R. and moves his hand to the door knob which falls off before he can reach it. In exasperation he gives the door a shove and it drops off its hinges. He shrugs and opens his mouth to shout, then stops and turns back to SUKEY.) I've just remembered - she's out anyway. It's not my day, is it?

SUKEY I don't think it ever is mine.

MUSIC 5. "MY DAY"

BILLY When I woke up it was pouring.
My throat hurt with snoring.

SUKEY I stubbed my toe on the wardrobe and I said "Hooray!"

BILLY There was no tea in the caddy;

SUKEY My egg was a baddy;

BOTH Then I began to suspect that this was not my day.

SUKEY All of the neighbours were grousin';

The cat brought a mouse in;

BILLY Postman brought seventeen bills that I forgot to pay.
When I resorted to satire
My bike got a flat tyre.

BOTH What with one thing and another it was not my day.
Since I could find no recompense
I thought I might change my residence
For somewhere sev'ral miles beneath the sea.

SUKEY Just then a miracle occurred -

BILLY I suddenly met a smashing bird -

BOTH And all at once it's lovely being me! WHEE!

SUKEY Why should I care if it's freezing,
My goldfish keeps sneezing?
Why should I worry if all my friends have run away?

BILLY I can be very much calmer -
I've just met a charmer!

BOTH And I've a shrewd suspicion this is just - my - day!

(Dance.)

I have been waiting for you, dear;
You've come right on cue, dear,
And I most earnestly hope that you have come to stay.
Since a good story line here is
Let's make it a series,
Then we'll be quite convinced that this is just our day.

BILLY You will stay, won't you?

SUKEY Rather!

BILLY Marvellous! I'll find mother and fix it up now. (Turns to go and falls over the ledgers.) Oh, blow these things.

SUKEY Never mind, I'll deal with them.

BILLY Jolly good. Just chuck 'em in Perkins and Perkins. (Points to office.) Shan't be a jiffy. (Runs off U.R.)

SUKEY (gathering up ledgers) Well I never, I'm his boss - one of them anyway. But bosses can't marry clerks. I know, I'll persuade Polly and we'll make him captain of "The Venturer". But then suppose he didn't want to marry me? How can one tell? (Throws ledgers over her shoulder.) He loves me, he loves me not, he loves me, he loves me not -

(MUSIC 6. POLLY PERKINS enters U.L.)

POLLY What are you doing, Sukey?

SUKEY Oh - er - book-keeping.

POLLY It looked more like book throwing away.

SUKEY (gathering up ledgers and putting them off into office) I was going through our accounts, Polly.

POLLY I didn't think our firm had any money worth accounting. I'm afraid our great-uncles who left it to us, weren't very good business men. Our only hope's a successful voyage with "The Venturer", so we must choose the right man for captain.

SUKEY Then I know just the man we need. His name's Bi - er - Mr Crusoe, and he's - he's - Oh, he really is, Polly. I'll find him and you can see for yourself.

POLLY Wait a minute, Sukey. Did you find anywhere for us to stay?

SUKEY Yes. There. (Points to house.) Much better than there. (Points to Inn.)

(The nameplate above house door slips down on one side.)

POLLY It is?

SUKEY Yes, but I think it's moulting or something. (She exits R.)

POLLY (laughing) Oh well, I suppose it might be quite cosy.

(The other end of the nameplate gives way.)

It's about as shaky as our firm. (Sighs.) And that would be much easier to run if only people would take young girls seriously in business. Of course a name like Polly Perkins doesn't help, not when you live in Paddington Green.

The hearty city gents just say, "Ah, pretty Polly, eh?" and expect me to blush once, giggle twice and then shut up. Well, I may be pretty, I hope I am, but that's not all I am.

MUSIC 7. "PRETTY"

Pretty.
They say my second name
Is pretty.
That is my claim to fame,
And I know
Good fortune smiles
Wherever I go,
Even a million miles.
But though
I'm sure it's very nice to know
That I can set some heart aglow
And to be beautiful is no disgrace,
Believe me I am not just a pretty face.

I have a purpose and I have a mind,
Under the surface a strength you will find.
And though
I'm sure it's very nice to know
That I can set some heart aglow
And to be beautiful is no disgrace,
Believe me I am not just a pretty face.

(She exits L.)

(MUSIC 8. Hooting off R. MRS CRUSOE enters U.R. on a child's scooter with a hooter and a shopping bag on the handlebars.)

MRS C. Stop! Stop! (Pulls on the handlebars like the reins of a horse.) Whoa back! WHOA! (She pulls so hard she falls over backwards, narrowly avoiding crashing into the Inn.) Ow! (She rises, rubbing her behind tenderly.) That's deflated my ego. I should have got the de luxe model with a brake. Anyway, thank goodness it didn't run into my house.

(Chimney pot falls off roof. MRS CRUSOE picks it up.)

There - just the thought's upset it. Still, what a blessing I forgot to order the chimney sweep. (Throws it off.)

Now I've told you that's my house I expect you've realised I'm Mrs Crusoe, haven't you? (Waits for reaction.) Well, haven't you? (Reaction.) That's better. I thought you would because you all look very intelligent. Don't you think they look intelligent, - (M.D.'s name)?

M.D. Oh, yes. The most intelligent audience we've had this performance.

MRS C. There, you can see he's intelligent too. Oh yes, he's not just a pretty face. Far from it. (Peers at him.) Yes, very far. He has got a lovely smile, though. Go on (name) turn round and dazzle them with those flashing white teeth. No, don't take 'em out, dear - just smile, you know.

(MUSICAL DIRECTOR turns to smile and bow to AUDIENCE.)

There, I felt a distinct quiver go through the whole place. Don't smile at my house, will you? (To AUDIENCE.) It looks a little shabby, I know, (Puts scooter off behind house.) but it's very comfy inside. H and C in every room - well, there has been since the boiler burst. And, of course, we've got a T.V. lounge. One day we'll have a T.V., too. My trouble is I take in the wrong sort of boarders - the ones without any money. Still I've managed to scrape enough together to buy a treat for my son, Robinson. Well, he's bound to have worked up a good appetite escaping. So I got him this. (Brings out a thin scraggy-looking chicken.) They told me it was a battery hen - I think it needs re-charging. It's left me skint, but never mind, I always say, something's bound to turn up - even if it's only the end of my nose.

<u>MUSIC 9.</u> "SOMETHING'S BOUND TO TURN UP"

Something's bound to turn up, to turn up, to turn up,
Something's bound to turn up, that's my philosophy.
Don't let life depress you. Good luck and God bless you.
Something's bound to turn up if you feel like me.
You will never do a thing
If you just sit grizz-l-ing
Smile a little smile and say
"Tomorrow is another day,"

And that's my raison d'etre –
(Can you say it bettre?) –
Something's bound to turn up if you feel
like me.

(Dance.)

Find in life the comic twist.
Don't become a pessimist.
People who look glum as hell
Make all of us feel bad as well,
So I'll be glad to lend 'em
My modus vivendum –
Something's bound to turn up if you feel like me!

(She exits into house. The lights fade to a single white spot focused U.R. MUSIC 10. BRITANNIA makes a stately entrance U.R. on rostrum dressed in the classic fashion and carrying a trident. When she gets D.C. she makes an imperious gesture to the M.D. with her trident and the music stops abruptly. She nods graciously.)

BRIT. I thank you for those few kind staves.
Yes, I am she who rules the waves,
Britannia, as I'm sure you've guess'd.
But now I'm on another quest,
And while I tell you of that task
I'll squat upon this handy cask.
(Sits on water butt by Inn.)
Now – I as Fairy Guardian serve
A lad of special pluck and nerve.
Who it is you won't have a clue so
I'll tell you now it's Robinson Crusoe!
I'm here his homecoming to bless;
And haply, from his vile duress,
He brings with him, the clever chap,
The Turkish pirate's treasure map,
Which will his future fortunes found.
'Tis safe to say this on dry ground
For my fell foeman, Davy Jones,
Who rules the underwater zones,
Can't exercise his powers here.
Indeed, just simply to appear
He needs some liquid medium handy

Like tea or coffee, rum or brandy;
And since there's not, he can't intrude.

(There is a FLASH and BRITANNIA is toppled off the cask as DAVY JONES lifts the lid and stands up. He looks like a disreputable edition of Neptune.)

DAVY That's where you're wrong!

BRIT. How very rude!

DAVY Ahoy, shipmate! What, on the deck?
Dear, dear, you look like some old wreck
That never more will go a-rovin',
Because it's had its bottom stove in!
(Guffaws heartily.)

BRIT. (rising with immense dignity)
A certain place is slightly bruis'd
And thus, to quote, we're not amus'd.
So kindly cease that ribald laughter
And tell me what you've come here after.

DAVY Aye, gladly, matey, since you ask.
While I a-floated in the cask
You showed me how you could be floor'd,
I'll break your power through your ward
And then I'll rule the sea and land!

BRIT. You never will! Not while I stand!
Meantime remember, Jones, that you
When on dry land are in the stew,
For if I empty out this butt
Your exit visa will go phut!

DAVY You wouldn't!

BRIT. Would!

DAVY (hurriedly lowering himself) All right, I'll go,
For now I'm powerless, I know.
But wait until I make my bid!

BRIT. You just be quiet and mind the lid.
(She bangs it down on him.)
Impertinence! But none the less
He could cause Robinson distress;
'Gainst which the best defence is love

And one who'll suit him like a glove
I have divin'd from mystic workin's
To be a certain Miss P. Perkins.
With her to help 'tis absolute
That he'll give Davy Jones the boot!

(She exits D.R. CHORUS assemble.)

MUSIC 11. "ANY MOMENT NOW"

CHORUS

If we wait a little longer
Robinson we soon will meet.
Any moment now we'll see him
Coming down the street.

Any moment, any moment, any moment now, now, now.
Any, any moment, any, any moment now, any moment now.
Any moment, any moment, any moment,
Now, now, now, now, now, now, now, now now!

(ROBINSON CRUSOE enters U.R. on rostrum and stops in C. while CHORUS crowd round below greeting him.)

MUSIC 12. "HOME AGAIN"

ROBINSON

If I told you all the things I've seen,
All the peoples, all the seas and palaces,
If you saw those azure skies you would not believe your eyes,
But I swear to you that it's true.
There were mountains you could climb for ever,
There were folk of ev'ry race and hue;
But now I have seen it all, still my fav'rite place of call
Is my home again, home with you.

I have sailed my way up mighty rivers,
Left my shadow on the tropic sands,
Where no man has ever been there's a place that I have seen;
Other hemispheres, other lands,
From the frozen poles to burning deserts,
I have crossed the old world and the new;

But now I have seen it all, still my fav'rite place of call
Is my home again, dear old home again,
My sweet home again, home with you.

(CHORUS disperse with temporary farewells. BILLY runs in R.)

BILLY Mother! Mother! He's coming! Any moment now he'll be - (Sees ROBINSON.) Oh. You are. But haven't you seen Mother yet? Mother! Mother! He's here! Robinson's here!

MRS C. (off R.) What? Oh, my boy! My boy! (She rushes blindly on with outstretched arms straight past ROBINSON and engulfs BILLY.) My long-lost son! To think I haven't seen you since - since - Oh, I don't know when.

BILLY I do. Breakfast time.

MRS C. Eh? Oh, wrong son. (Drops BILLY and turns to ROBINSON.) Ah, there's my Robinson. Ooh, I feel all faint. (She flops into BILLY's arms and he struggles to hold her up.) It's too much for me.

BILLY It's too much for me, too.

MRS C. (recovering) Then I'll faint somewhere more comfortable later. (Hugs ROBINSON.) Oh, it's lovely to have you home again, dear.

ROBINSON It's lovely to be home, mother.

(One end of the window sill on the house gives way and the flower pots slide to the ground.)

BILLY You're only just in time. It can't stand the excitement.

ROBINSON Never mind. (He brings out a folded up treasure map.) I got something from the Turk when I escaped that might help us buy another. Several, in fact. It's a map of an island showing where his buried treasure lies.

MRS C. Oooh, how exciting! And is it a nice handy island - like the Isle of Wight, say?

ROBINSON No, it's in the Caribbean.

BILLY — That's lucky, "The Venturer's" bound for the West Indies. The owners are picking a crew today.

ROBINSON — (putting map away) Splendid. Then somehow I must be one of them.

(Loud squawk off R.)

MRS C. — Oh listen, we're forgetting that parrot of yours. He's been almost as excited as we have.

BILLY — I'll go and let him off his perch. (Exits into house.)

ROBINSON — Good old Broody. I've got some very special sunflower seeds for him. (Brings out a bag.)

MRS C. — Ah, he'll love those. But don't let him have them all at once, dear. He seems to have grown rather a lot lately.

(MUSIC 13. BROODY puts his head on from house.)

BROODY — Hullo! hullo! hullo! (He runs to ROBINSON.)

(BILLY follows sucking his finger.)

ROBINSON — Oh yes, you have grown, Broody!

BILLY — Yes, and I wish he wouldn't think he can still perch on my finger.

BROODY — There's a lovely bird! (Puts his head down for ROBINSON to scratch.)

ROBINSON — (scratching his head) Yes, you are a lovely bird.

(BROODY flutters his wings. A window shutter falls off house.)

MRS C. — No, no, stop that Broody. You'll blow the house down with the state it's in.

(BROODY cackles with laughter and flutters more. Second window shutter falls.)

No, no, naughty. Naughty, Polly!

(BROODY stops with an angry squawk.)

ROBINSON — Ah, he still doesn't like being called Polly, eh? Never mind, Broody. Look what I've got for you - sunflower seeds.

(BROODY gratefully rubs his head against ROBINSON and plunges his beak into the bag.)

MRS C. Careful, he'll have the lot.

ROBINSON (tugging at bag) I can't get it away!

(MRS CRUSOE grabs hold of BROODY and BILLY grasps ROBINSON's waist. After a short tug o' war BROODY is suddenly pulled away causing MRS CRUSOE and BILLY to fall. ROBINSON looks in bag and brings out one seed.)

There's only one left.

(BROODY tries to snatch it.)

Oh, Broody, how can you be so greedy?

BILLY I think he finds it quite easy.

MRS C. You silly thing, Broody. If we'd planted a few of those we could have grown you some more seeds.

BILLY (taking seed) Well, let's plant this one in this pot over here. (Plants it in pot by L. pros. arch.) Of course, it'll be some time before it comes up.

(Music whizz and a sunflower plant shoots out of pot.)

Golly!

MRS C. Yes, what a surprise. (To AUDIENCE.) I bet you never thought that would happen. (Reaction.) Oh no, you didn't. (Reaction.) Oh no, you didn't. (Reaction.) Well, maybe you did.

(BROODY starts to edge surreptitiously towards plant.)

ROBINSON I told you they were special seeds.

MRS C. It's a pity that pot's over the road from our house, but I don't suppose anybody will try to take it.

BILLY No.

ROBINSON Oh no.

ALL THREE NO.

(They turn and see that BROODY is just about to.)

Broody!

(BROODY scuttles away.)

BILLY I've got it! A brainwave. Listen. (He whispers quickly to others.)

MRS C. Well! However did you think of a thing like that? (To AUDIENCE.) This will gast your flabbers to the utmost. We're going to ask you to look after it!

ROBINSON We want you to shout, "Sunflower!" if you see anybody try to take it.

BILLY It's rather a novelty though, isn't it? I think we ought to practise it. (To AUDIENCE.) We'll hide and you shout when Broody pretends to take it.

(BROODY cackles with laughter.)

ALL THREE Pretend, Broody!

(MRS CRUSOE runs off D.R., BILLY U.L. and ROBINSON U.R. BROODY creeps to flower. When the AUDIENCE shout he stops and they look on.)

MRS C. Have they done it yet?

ROBINSON I didn't hear anything.

BILLY Nor did I.

MRS C. Let's hide again.

(They disappear. BROODY creeps to plant and stops as before when AUDIENCE shout. Others look on.)

ROBINSON There was a whisper.

MRS C. A murmur.

BILLY A faint susurration.

MRS C. Ooh! One more time.

(The business is repeated as before and they run on.)

ROBINSON A shout!

BILLY A bellow!

MRS C. A veritable vociferation! - if you'll pardon the expression. And now we know it's quite safe. I'm a bit parched, though. Let's go and have a cuppa.

BILLY Righto, mother. I'll put the kettle on the candle.

MRS C. Oh, use two candles today, dear, and blow the expense.

(They exit into house.)

ROBINSON Come on, Broody. I don't trust you out here with that sunflower.

(BROODY is outraged.)

It's no use pretending to be innocent, I know you better. Come on. (Moves towards him.)

(BROODY squawks and moves a sidestep to L.)

Broody!

(BROODY moves another sidestep L.)

Well, I'll take you in then.

(BROODY squawks and runs off L. flapping his wings. ROBINSON runs after him.)

Hey, come back! (Off L.) All right, I shall call you Polly.

(POLLY PERKINS enters U.R.)

POLLY I wonder if Sukey's Mr Crusoe is here now.

ROBINSON (off L.) Pretty Polly! Pretty Polly!

POLLY Well, really!

ROBINSON (off) There's a lovely bird.

POLLY How dare he!

ROBINSON (off) Yes, you are. You're a lovely bird, Polly.

POLLY (moving purposefully L.) I'll soon deal with him.

ROBINSON (putting his head on to look round Inn wing) Where are you, Polly?

POLLY I'm here!

ROBINSON Eh? (Turns head and sees her.) Oh. (Enters fully.) I beg your pardon?

POLLY And so you ought.

ROBINSON Ought I? Oh. (Calls to L.) Broody!

POLLY I am not broody!

ROBINSON No, I know. Broody's my parrot, I was just calling him.

POLLY Then why were you calling me too?

ROBINSON Oh, but I wasn't.

POLLY Yes, you were - Pretty Polly.

ROBINSON Where?

POLLY Here! I am!

ROBINSON Oh! You mean your name really is Polly. No wonder you were cross. I was only calling "Polly" to tease my parrot. You do believe me, don't you?

POLLY I might - if I was sure you really had a parrot.

(BROODY runs on L. with a loud squawk.)

Oh, yes. You have got a parrot.

ROBINSON Broody, you naughty boy. You made this lady think I was insulting her. Now say "How do you do" to her nicely.

(BROODY puts his head on one side fixing her with his beady eye for a moment then gives a raucous wolf whistle.)

Broody!

(BROODY runs off into house chortling parrot chuckles highly pleased with himself. POLLY laughs.)

I'm sorry about that.

POLLY Never mind. But is that where you live? You see, I came here looking for a Mr Crusoe.

ROBINSON Did you? Good! Here I am - Robinson Crusoe. But why were you looking for me?

POLLY My sister thinks you're just the man we need.

ROBINSON Really? I hope she's right - Polly. And you know, you really are a pretty Polly; though I suppose you get tired of people telling you that.

POLLY Yes, very tired. Please say it again.

ROBINSON Pretty Polly.

MUSIC 14. "PRETTY POLLY"

Pretty Polly, Pretty Polly! Such a lovely name;
To call you any other would be an awful shame.

POLLY When they call'd me Pretty Polly I was most distressed,
But now I hear you speak it, I think I like it best.

BOTH What made my heart burst into flame
When first you came in view?

POLLY Was it the way you spoke my name?

ROBINSON The lovely name of you?

POLLY Could you love a girl call'd Polly?

ROBINSON I could surely try!

BOTH Then as we love each other, and all the years go by,
I'll love the name of Polly till I die.

(ROBINSON exits into house and POLLY U.L. MUSIC 15. WILL ATKINS enters U.R. on rostrum.)

WILL Ha-ha! He-he! Ho-ho! and likewise, hum-hum! There she is - "The Venturer", my chance to be a captain at last. Captain Will Atkins! What a mellifluous ring that has. It's worth another little laugh. Ha-ha! He-he! Ho-ho! Oh no. I'm straining my voice. (Takes out a throat spray and sprays throat.) That's better. Ah, what delicious villainies would be open to me as captain of "The Venturer". I could flog the cargo, flog the crew - if they like that sort of thing - and even flog the - er-hm - flog the - hrrm. I've got a flog in my throat. (Quickly sprays throat again and puts spray away.) Yes, even flog the whole ship. And surely the owners are bound to choose me as captain; especially since I fixed Robinson Crusoe, but I'd better keep mum about that - ah, if only I could keep Mum, his Mum, my little Letitia! Easy, the old ticker's over palpitating. (Brings out a bottle of pills.) Control yourself, Will, you love-crazy loon. (Swallows pills and shudders.) Yeuk! Yes. I must keep my mind on

"The Venturer". Now, do I look smart enough? (Sees sunflower.) That's an idea, a nice flower for my buttonhole. I'll take it. (He moves to take it.)

(AUDIENCE shout.)

What's going on? Noises in my head now!

(MRS CRUSOE runs out of house with a bass broom.)

MRS C. Thank you. Take that, you sunflower snitcher! (She buffets him in his midriff with broom causing him to crumple.)

WILL Ooh! My ulcer!

MRS C. You pot-plant pincher! (She hits his bent over rear so that he falls flat.)

WILL Ow! My - my-my!

MRS C. (banging up and down the length of him) And it's lucky for you my son Robinson returned home today or I wouldn't be in such a good mood.

WILL (attempting to rise) What!

MRS C. You heard, you botany bagger! (She bangs him down again and exits into house.)

WILL That was my secret love. But somehow I don't think she recognized me. (Twirling moustache.) That's because of my crafty disguise. (Rising and feeling himself tenderly.) Ooh! Really, villainy's very taxing. Ah, if only Letitia hadn't turned me down I might never have become a villain. You see, when she chose Robinson's father, instead of me, I took it very badly. Well, I had a nasty cold at the time, I remember. And when he died I vowed vengeance on Robinson's head - and anywhere else that was handy. That's why I bribed a Turkish pirate to take him prisoner. Now he's ruined everything by escaping! Oh, it's enough to drive a man to drink. (He takes out a flask.) The trouble is, I hate the stuff - well, it gives me such indigestion. Still, I must make an effort. They told me this has some really strong gin in it.

(As he uncorks flask and prepares to take a swig there is a

FLASH, BLACKOUT, LIGHTS UP and DAVY JONES is standing on his L.)

Well, either I am in "Aladdin",
Or this was rotten gin they had in -
You get D.T.s before you drink!

DAVY Easy, shipmate, 'taint like you think.

WILL Who are you then?

DAVY Why, Davy Jones.

WILL That's sent a shudder through my bones.
In fact upon a quick prognosis
You've caused a cardiac thrombosis!
(He rolls about the stage clutching his heart in a vociferous ecstasy of pain.)

DAVY My words perhaps will prove a balm,
For 'tisn't you I'd bring to harm.
I've come to tell you how to do so
To a certain Master Crusoe.

WILL Aha! You mean, we're allies?

DAVY Snap!

WILL How then?

DAVY He has a treasure map,
That's of a far West Indies isle.
"The Venturer's" bound there in short while
So he intends to sail with her;
Could you somehow his plans - deter?

WILL Well, yes indeed. Now let me think
Ah, this might help.
(He is about to take a swig.)

DAVY No, wait, don't drink!
I'll not get home without a drop.

WILL Suppose the lad I cannot stop?

DAVY Ah, I can't help you more on land,
At sea, though, I've a freer hand.
But now, I'm getting too dried out.
So pull the stopper from the spout.

Farewell, and best of British luck.

WILL Thank you. (Pulls cork from flask and looks at narrow opening.) You sure you won't get stuck?

(DAVY gives a hearty laugh. There is a FLASH, BLACKOUT - during which DAVY exits - and LIGHTS UP.)

(coughing hard) Hasn't he heard of the clean air act? (Turns flask upside down and sees it is empty.) Um - thirsty chap. Never mind, I'll fill it up again in there, for already a dastardly scheme forms in my mind and that's just the place to find the filthy sea scum I need to carry it out. Ha-ha! He-he! Ho-ho! Hum-OW! (He crashes into Inn piece, and goes off L. holding his nose.) Landlord! Bring me a double Elastoplast!

MALE VOICE (off R.) Come in, number four! (Slight pause. More urgently.) Come in, number four!

(MUSIC 16. A cut-out of a child's paddle boat, plainly numbered "4", fore and aft, appears R. behind the quay with JOLLY ROGER apparently sitting at his ease in the bows facing aft where RUEFUL RUPERT apparently sits facing for'ard paddling furiously with his R. hand. (The cut-out is, in fact, carried on by them with ROGER walking backwards.))

(very indignantly) COME IN, NUMBER FOUR!

ROGER Never! Never! We'll show 'em our true colours! (Brings his R. hand up grasping a cutlass, with a Skull and Crossbones flag attached to it.) There! Number Four will never come in again! (He thrusts the cutlass into the deck of the boat - that is into a hole in the centre of RUPERT's strut.)

(Sound of splintering wood on ratchet from Drummer. They gradually lower themselves and the cut-out so that it looks as if the craft is sinking.)

RUPERT I don't think you should have done that, Roger.

ROGER Why not, Rupert? (Realises his head is now on a level with quayside.) Oh. (Bellows.) Abandon ship!

(Both scramble onto quay and look back to where their boat has disappeared.)

Pity. Never mind, Rupert, at least we're real pirates now. We have committed an act of piracy on the high seas.

RUPERT I thought it was on the boating pool.

ROGER Well - everybody has to start somewhere. Today the boating pool, tomorrow -

RUPERT Prison.

ROGER Yes. No! Don't you understand, Rupert, from now on life is just a bowl of cherries. All we have to do is eat them.

RUPERT But if I eat too many I'll be sick. But that's just like life - it makes you sick.

ROGER Don't be so rueful, Rupert.

RUPERT Well, you're so jolly, Roger.

ROGER That's it! That can be our trade name - Jolly Roger and Rueful Rupert, Hire Service Pirates. Meanwhile I've got a little sideline for us to raise some lolly. (He takes some large pieces of white card from a bag slung over his shoulder.) There! (He displays them proudly. They are headed, "GENUINE PIRATE TREASURE MAP", below which is a perfect circle with an "X" in the middle of it.) Good, eh?

RUPERT Hm. Don't you think somebody might see through them?

ROGER Oh, no. I used very thick cardboard. Now we need some customers.

(WILL enters L. from Inn sniffing a large prop smelling salts bottle.)

WILL Phew! Beastly stuffy place. All I found was a headache; not a sign of any filthy sea scum. But somehow I must get hold of that treasure map.

ROGER Rupert! You hear that? Our first cherry!

RUPERT You mean we've got to eat him?

ROGER No, no, he wants a treasure map. Well, sell him one.

RUPERT (doubtfully) I'll try. (Crosses to WILL and nudges him to attract his attention.) Hullo, cherry.

WILL I beg your pardon?

RUPERT I said, hullo cherry. (Proffers a map.) Would you like a -

WILL How dare you! Go away!

RUPERT (crossing back) He's a sour cherry.

ROGER Well, you've definitely given him the pip.

WILL Filthy sea scum! Ah, filthy sea scum. Er - maybe you could help me. It's a little matter of a treasure map.

ROGER Ah, you see, Rupert? Just a bit of sales resistance. (To WILL.) A treasure map, of course. (Offers him a selection.) Which one would you like?

WILL Eh? Not this trash -

ROGER Trash?

WILL I'm after a real one from a bloke called Robinson Crusoe who lives over there. I want you to set on him and take it.

ROGER We're not common footpads, you know. We're real pirates, registered at Lloyds.

WILL All right then, I want you to board him and take his booty.

RUPERT Which booty? His left booty or his right booty?

ROGER No, no, Rupert, the treasure map's his booty.

RUPERT Oh, a sort of kinky booty.

WILL What do you say, lads? I'll pay well.

BOTH We're on.

WILL Good! I'll wait for you in there - even though it means another splitting head. (Goes off to Inn.) Landlord, bring me a large aspirin and Alka-Seltzer.

ROGER Right, Rupert, I've thought of a plan to lure this Crusoe out here. We'll send him some flowers with a note saying they're from his sweetheart who wants to meet him here now.

RUPERT But we haven't any flowers.

ROGER Well, here's one for a start. We'll take that.

(They move towards sunflower. AUDIENCE shout and

BILLY runs out of house.)

BILLY Hullo, hullo, hullo! Trying to nick our sunflower, eh?

ROGER Yours? I'm sorry, we didn't know that, Mr - er, Mr -

BILLY Crusoe.

ROGER Mr Crusoe - Crusoe?

BILLY Crusoe.

ROGER & RUPERT Crusoe!

ROGER What a bit of luck. (Nods at RUPERT and they pull pop-guns from their belts.) Now hand over your treasure map or we'll blast you full of cork.

BILLY But I haven't got a treasure map.

ROGER Oh. How awkward.

RUPERT (putting pop-gun away) Well, that's that then.

ROGER No, I know, Rupert - we'll sell him one of ours.

BILLY You won't. I haven't any money.

ROGER Tt-tt, life's full of little difficulties, isn't it? We'll lend you some then. Rupert, lend him 2p.

RUPERT Yes, I knew it'd be me. (Gives BILLY a coin.) There you are.

ROGER Now you give it to me.

(BILLY does and ROGER pockets coin.)

RUPERT Hey, that's -

ROGER Ssh, Rupert, give him a map. After all, he's paid for it.

(RUPERT does so.)

There, now you have got a treasure map, haven't you?

BILLY Yes.

ROGER (levelling pop-gun at him again. Toughly) Then hand it over!

BILLY (shrugging, mystified) All right. (He does.)

ROGER — Thank you. (Puts pop-gun away and strides to Inn.) Very satisfactory. Come, Rupert.

RUPERT — (following puzzled) I think there's something wrong somewhere.

(They exit into Inn.)

BILLY — I wonder what that was all about?

(EFFECT 2. A clock begins to chime and then strike 12.)

Noon - Perkins and Perkins - the accounts! Too late. I'd better try and look efficient, anyway.

(He takes out a scroll of paper and a large quill pen as the CHORUS begin to assemble with a buzz of chatter and ROBINSON comes out of house.)

Now, who's here? (Starts to write, the quill keeps hitting his nose as he does.) Robinson, good and you - and you - and you - and - and - achoo! And who isn't here? Come on, hands up anyone who isn't here.

(CHORUS laugh.)

ROBINSON — I know who isn't here, Billy - Perkins and Perkins.

(POLLY and SUKEY enter U.L. on rostrum.)

POLLY & SUKEY — Oh, yes we are.

(General surprise.)

BILLY — You, Sukey?) Together

ROBINSON — You, Polly?)

POLLY — The Misses Perkins -

SUKEY — If you please.

(They soften their formality with broad winks, POLLY to ROBINSON, SUKEY to BILLY.)

POLLY — Our ship, "The Venturer", is ready to sail as soon as there's a crew aboard. And our choice of Captain is -

(WILL runs out of Inn chasing a protesting ROGER and RUPERT.)

WILL You extra filthy sea-scum! (Throws their treasure map at them.) You're useless!

BILLY Ssh! The owners are just announcing the Captain.

WILL What? (Preens himself.) Oh, of course. I expect they've been waiting till I got here to say that it's -

POLLY It's Robinson Crusoe.

(MRS CRUSOE enters as the announcement is being made, carrying a large packet of Kwells.)

CHORUS Hurray!)

ROBINSON Thank you, ladies.)

WILL Curses!) (Together.)

SUKEY Oh no!)

MRS C. Well done, dear! And it's a long trip so I've brought you some Kwells.

SUKEY Well, what about the first mate? I think -

ROBINSON Will Atkins and I have sailed together before. I'd be pleased to have him.

POLLY Of course.

ROBINSON All right, Will?

WILL Delighted! (Aside.) Impudent pipsqueak. I must look out for another Turkish pirate.

SUKEY Then Billy must be the second mate. I insist.

BILLY Do you? Oh, jolly good.

ROGER What about us?

WILL You! You rotten, incompetent - (Aside.) Wait, they might be useful. (To others.) As I was saying a couple of excellent deck hands.

ROBINSON Any other volunteers?

MALE CHORUS Aye, aye, sir!

GIRLS And us.

ROBINSON You?

1st GIRL Yes. If my man wants a wife in every port it'll be the one he takes with him - me!

GIRLS Here, here!

ROBINSON But the owners wouldn't like me to take women aboard.

POLLY Oh yes, we would, Captain.

SUKEY We've just decided we're going too.

MRS C. Well, blow me down! I'd go meself only I can't leave the old homestead.

(The porch canopy falls down on one side.)

It looks as if the old homestead's leaving me. I will go!

POLLY Bravo, Mrs Crusoe. Any more?

(BROODY runs squawking out of house in a sailor hat. All laugh.)

ROBINSON Good old, Broody! Then all aboard and cast off!

ALL Aye, aye, Cap'n!

MUSIC 17. "HEAVE HO!" (Reprise)

(During the number all get on board, the rope is released from the bollard, we see the anchor rise, then slowly the ship moves L.)

Heave ho! We've got a ship,
And at long, long last we set out to sea.
We are off on a trip,
And it's just the way it ought to be.
Our "Venturer" is in commission,
In a mainly good condition.
We are pleased with our position
On this happy day.
Shed no tears for our parting,
Our adventure is starting.
Tide is right and the weather's fine;
We're loaded down to the plimsoll line -
So cut the talk and let's get under way!

(BLACKOUT. Close traverse tabs. Fly in Scene 2 frontcloth.)

Scene 2 'Tween Decks on "The Venturer"

Open tabs when ready during scene to reveal a frontcloth of a lower deck. The sunflower is drooping.

LIGHTS UP. MUSIC 18. BRITANNIA enters R.

BRIT. So far I'm glad to say, all's well.
(The cloth starts to sway from side to side. She sways in contrary motion to it.)
But what is this, an ocean swell?
I order'd calm seas all the way;
You naughty waves, be still I say!
(She makes an imperious gesture with her trident and the cloth stops.)
That's Davy Jones, the silly goat,
How just like him to rock the boat.
So I must keep a special watch
Or here at sea my plans he'll botch.
(Notices sunflower.)
Tut-tut, that plant looks most forlorn,
I'll summon help ere it's quite gorn.
I'll seem to take it for my bower,
(Moves towards it.)
And that will make you shout -

AUDIENCE Sunflower!

MRS C. (off L.) Coming! Just coming!

BRIT. (moving R.) Oh, well done.

(MRS CRUSOE runs on L.)

MRS C. Ah, caught you, eh? No use to run,
For it's distinctive if not subtle
To wear a nightie and a scuttle.

(BRITANNIA is motioning toward plant with her trident.)

And what you doing with that fork?

BRIT. I'm pointing out your droopy stalk.

MRS C. My what - (Looks at plant.) Oh, yes I see. I say!

I'll deal with that without delay.

BRIT. I thought you might, so off I'll trot
Now that your plant won't go to pot.
(She exits R.)

MRS C. What a witty lady. I wonder who she was? Anyway, I've got just the thing for the sunflower here. (Brings from off L. a huge bottle labelled "WHIFFINURE".) There, some Whiffinure, it's a liquid fertiliser. Percy Thrower threw it at me so it must be good. (Looks at label.) "Apply liberally." Well, I'll give it the lot. I expect it's got something special in it. (Removes stopper and starts to pour into plant pot.)

(FLASH, BLACKOUT, LIGHTS UP and DAVY JONES has entered beside her. The sunflower has straightened up.)

My, my! It's tricky stuff to use!
It's cur'd the plant but blown a fuse!
And what a smell without the cork.

(DAVY prods her behind with his trident.)

Ow! What was that? (Looks round.) Another fork!

DAVY A trident, ma'am, 'mongst sailor men.

MRS C. Well, don't "try dent"-ing me again!
Oh really, I can't stand this pooh.
(Moves to DAVY.)
Perhaps it's better here by - OOH!
(Staggers back from him.)

DAVY (sniffs at his arm and is rather staggered himself. Aside)
Cor! I've the fertiliser's pong!

MRS C. Who are you then that you're so - strong?

DAVY (thinking hard)
We-ll - bilge pipe cleaning is my duty.

MRS C. No wonder then you're rather fruity,
And so you'll understand my urge
To give my nose a thorough purge.
Besides, it's time to bed I slunk,
In other words - I'm going to bunk! (She exits L.)

DAVY Can't say I blame her, poor old duck,

But then I had to take pot luck
To get aboard the ship somehow
And see what Will is planning now
To fix young Crusoe. Ah, Will's coming.

(Enter WILL ATKINS R., gleefully rubbing his hands.)

WILL Ha-ha! He-he! Well, things are humming!
(Notices smell and reacts.)
I'll say they are! What can it be?

DAVY (stepping forward)
Don't fret, my hearty, it's just me.
The stuff I came by's rather chronic.

WILL My sinuses will need a tonic.
But just for now, as you're so crudey,
(Takes out a clothes-peg and clips it on his nose.)
I'll have to talk like Punch and Judy.

DAVY You've got a plan then, matey?

WILL Natch!
I have come here a plot to hatch
By which the ship and map I'll seize.
I can't say more or else I'll sneeze.

DAVY On my help, shipmate, you can bank
If you make Crusoe walk the plank.
Once in the waves I'll drag him down
To reach my Locker and to drown!
(Places an arm confidentially round WILL's shoulder.)
And then - (Smells his arm thus placed.)
Have you another peg?
I'm worser than a rotten egg.

(WILL shakes his head.)

Then I must leave you for the sea,
I'm getting too much now for me!

(FLASH. BLACKOUT. DAVY exits. LIGHTS UP.)

WILL Helpful chap, but I do wish he'd give up smoking.
(Takes peg off.) Oh, I can take this off, can't I?
Ooh, my mucous membranes. Now, where are those two
pirates so I can plan my mutiny?

(ROGER puts his head on L. and RUPERT his R.)

BOTH Hist!

WILL Aah! My nerves! Don't do that. Come over here. I want to plot a plot.

(MUSIC 19. They move onstage and assume conspiratorial positions.)

Listen carefully. We meet at the poop deck at eight bells tomorrow. Got that?

BOTH Got that.

WILL And you must foregather with your arms concealed about you.

RUPERT Ooh. Where are we going to put them then?

ROGER Simple, Rupert, we just shove 'em down our trousers. (Puts his arms down his trousers.)

WILL Yes, you just shove. No, you do not shove 'em down your trousers. I'm not talking about those arms. I mean your side arms.

RUPERT (looking at his arms) But these are side arms.

ROGER Yes, there'd be something wrong with us if we had front and back arms.

WILL Not those arms at all! Your weapons - cutlasses, daggers, pistols, these things! (He tugs at the pop-gun in RUPERT's belt and it goes off.) Oh, sorry. I didn't know it was loaded. Anyway, you bring them with you, but don't let anybody see them.

ROGER And what happens then?

WILL We seize the ship, blindfold Crusoe and force him to walk the plank. But you'll have to do that bit. I can't bear to see anybody suffer.

ROGER Oh, neither can I.

RUPERT Nor me.

WILL All right, we'll blindfold ourselves and then force him to walk the plank. Anyway, at eight bells tomorrow we moot at the peep deck. I mean we poot at the meet deck.

Er-hm. We - deck - at - the - the - meet - poop, poop at the deck meet, peek at the deep moot - aah! Careful, Will, you haven't time for a nervous breakdown now. We'll meet at the wheelhouse. Ooh, I'm quite looking forward to it.

ROGER Ooh, so am I.

RUPERT Ooh - I'm not. Eight bells cuts right across our tea break.

<u>MUSIC 20.</u> "BLUES"

(Close traverse tabs and fly out frontcloth during number.)

ALL You see before you a naughty trio,
We only play to win.

ROGER I take advantage.

RUPERT I take the orders.

WILL I take my medicine.

ALL Anyone who's available is going to get a basinful
Of Deep Sea Blues.

We're very wicked, we get you worried,
We give you aches and chills.

ROGER I take no nonsense.

RUPERT I take no notice.

WILL I take my lovely pills.

ALL Anyone who our art employs is giving the Wavy
Navy boys
The Navy Blues.

ROGER We'll do the beating when you face the music.

RUPERT We'll dot your crotchets in ev'ry bar.

BOTH We'll give you allegro con molto mosso -

WILL I've seen that inside my doctor's encyclopaedia.

ALL We're in a hurry, if you would pass us
You'll have to be darned quick.

ROGER I'm going places.

RUPERT I'm going with you.

WILL I'm going to be sick.

ALL No matter where or when it is, we're going to give our enemies
The Black and Blues.

(BLACKOUT. Open traverse tabs.)

Scene 3 The Main Deck of "The Venturer"

Fullset. Cut-out of the stern at the back of the rostrum, a ship's wheel C. on the rostrum and railing along the front of the rostrum between companion-way steps going down L.C. and R.C. Wings L. and R. of bulwarks and rigging. In C. below the rostrum a mainmast rises with stays going out to the bulwarks, and a border at the top of it represents a sail. U.L. is a large cask labelled "RUM". If feasible a cloud projector moves clouds slowly across the cyc.

The CHORUS as SAILORS and SAILORESSES are discovered, also ROBINSON, MRS CRUSOE, BILLY and SUKEY in a line in front of them.

MUSIC 21. "SAILORS' CHORES"

ALL If you decide to go off to sea
With hardened seamen such as we,
There's one little fact we are giving you -
There's lots of work to do.

ROBINSON (with scrubbing action)
Rub and scrub with a holystone!

(ROGER and RUPERT enter L. and observe the OTHERS as they repeat the line and copy the action.)

OTHERS Rub and scrub with a holystone!

If you decide, etc.

(At the end of the refrain ROGER and RUPERT move in front

of the PRINCIPALS and prepare to holystone.)

MRS C. (stepping forward with a kick)
Wakey! Wakey! Show a leg!

OTHERS Wakey! Wakey! Show a leg!

(Their action results in ROGER and RUPERT being kicked.)

Rub and scrub with a holystone!

If you decide, etc.

(By the end of this refrain ROGER and RUPERT have positioned themselves at either end of the PRINCIPALS' line, and are preparing to show a leg.)

BILLY (twirling his arm then flinging it out to one side)
Twirl the line and heave the log!

OTHERS Twirl the line and heave the log!

(This results in ROGER and RUPERT being struck by the outflung arms of those on the ends of the line.)

Wakey! Wakey! Show a leg!
Rub and scrub with a holystone!

If you decide, etc.

(During the refrain ROGER and RUPERT move into the C. of the line.)

SUKEY (pushing with her arms and circling round)
Turn the capstan round we go!

OTHERS Turn the capstan round we go!

(This results in ROGER and RUPERT being buffeted in their stomachs and pushed round to the ends of the line, where they are again struck as the others continue.)

Twirl the line and heave the log!
Wakey! Wakey! Show a leg!
Rub and scrub with a holystone!

If you decide, etc.

(At the end of this refrain ALL turn to ROGER and RUPERT, who have worked themselves in front of the line, waiting for their contribution.)

ROGER & RUPERT — Dance the hornpipe on the deck!

(In doing so they collide, as the others copy them they ALL collide with them.)

OTHERS — Dance the hornpipe on the deck!

(During the following everything happens to ROGER and RUPERT so that they are prostrate by the end of the number.)

Turn the capstan round we go!
Twirl the line and heave the log!
Wakey! Wakey! Show a leg!
Rub and scrub with a holystone!
One little fact we're giving you -
There's lots of work to do,
There's lots of work to do.

RUPERT — Ooh, aren't sailors rough?

(They stagger to one side. One of the SAILORS takes up a position behind the wheel. EFFECT 3. Six bells sound off.)

MRS C. — Well, that's exhausted me, Captain dear. I think I'll take it easy with a spot of sunbathing.

BILLY — Me too. I didn't get a wink of sleep last night. I think my hammock needs darning. It's full of holes.

MRS C. — Oh no, dear, that's what hammocks are - a lot of holes held together by string.

(They exit R.)

ROBINSON — The wind's veering south, Mr Mate. Reef the tops'ls, and take her two points starboard.

WILL — Aye, sir. Two points starboard!

HELMSMAN — Two points starboard! (Turns the wheel to R.)) (Together.)

WILL — You men, up aloft to hitch those tops'ls!)

4 MALE CH. — Aye, aye, sir! (They run off.)

WILL — And you men - er, lads - er, women's lib party, report to the galley!

GIRLS — Aye, aye, sir! (They run off.)

ROBINSON I'm going below. Take over, if you please, Mr Atkins. (He exits R.)

WILL Aye, sir. Jumped up Jackanapes! Little does he know how much I'll be taking over. Meanwhile, you lads can -

(BROODY strides on D.L. on a long leash, the other end of which is held by SUKEY.)

BROODY Man the guns!

ROGER & RUPERT Man the guns! (They run to one side.)

WILL Stop!

(They do. BROODY exits D.R.)

SUKEY Sorry. Can't stop. Taking Broody for a walk. (She is yanked off R.)

RUPERT She's taking Broody?

WILL You lads can -

BROODY (returning D.R. and striding back L.) Shiver me timbers!

ROGER & RUPERT (picking up WILL and shaking him) Shiver your timbers!

(SUKEY trails after BROODY as he exits L.)

SUKEY Not so fast! (She is yanked off L.)

WILL Put me down!

(They do.)

Just for that you can empty the swill buckets, but mind which way the wind's blowing. I must compose myself for the mutiny with a tranquiliser. (He exits R.)

ROGER Isn't it exciting, Rupert?

RUPERT What, emptying the swill buckets?

ROGER No, all this nautical stuff. Reef the tops'ls, two points starboard.

HELMSMAN Two points starboard! (Turns wheel R.)

(ROGER and RUPERT stagger R.)

ROGER Oh, no! Two points - er - the other way.

HELMSMAN Two points the other way. (Turns wheel L.)

(ROGER and RUPERT stagger L.)

WILL (looking back from hatchway) What's happening?

ROGER Nothing, Mr Atkins. We just - er - skidded.

WILL Skidded?

ROGER Yes, the sea's very wet and slippery today.

(ROGER and RUPERT run off L.)

WILL Humph! (Goes off R.)

(BILLY and MRS CRUSOE enter R. each carrying a deck chair and wearing comic bathing costumes.)

MRS C. (stopping R.C.) Do you like the costume? I got it for a ridiculous figure.

BILLY Yes, it looks as if you've been poured into it - and forgotten when to say stop.

(They set up their chairs R.C. and settle down.)

Ah, this is the life, eh?

(As MRS CRUSOE continues, ROGER and RUPERT enter L., with two large wooden buckets each. Both put one down in C. and RUPERT continues to R., behind the deck chairs, and flings the contents of his bucket over the R. bulwark.)

MRS C. Yes, dear, and there's a nice little breeze blowing in our faces.

(A lot of rubbish is thrown on from R., to land on MRS CRUSOE and BILLY.)

BILLY There's something else blowing in our faces.

MRS C. Let's go over here, then.

(They move their chairs to L.C. As they cross they nod to ROGER, who hurriedly puts his bucket behind his back. RUPERT gathers up the rubbish into his bucket again.)

RUPERT (aside) We forgot to mind which way the wind's blowing like Mr Atkins said. We'd better chuck the stuff this side.

(BROODY enters L. and strides across to R., the leash is now trailing behind him.)

BROODY Hard-a-port!

HELMSMAN Hard-a-port! (Turns wheel to L.)

(ROGER and RUPERT stagger L., MRS CRUSOE and BILLY lurch L. in their chairs.)

ALL Whoops!

MRS C. Now there's a nice breeze here, too.

(ROGER throws his rubbish off L. behind the deck chairs. It is thrown back on to land over MRS CRUSOE and BILLY.)

BILLY Perhaps somebody forgot to give the dustmen their Christmas tip.

RUPERT Shall I throw my bucket now?

ROGER No!

MRS C. Oh, it's you two. You silly things, you have to see which way the wind's blowing.

ROGER & RUPERT How?

BILLY Suck it and see. (He moistens a finger and holds it up.) And it's blowing from there now. (Points L.)

(BROODY returns D.R. and moves U.S.)

BROODY Hard-a-starboard! (Hides behind mast.)

HELMSMAN Hard-a-starboard! (Turns wheel to R.)

ALL (staggering to R.) Whoops!

MRS C. & BILLY (picking up the buckets in C.) So you throw it here. (They throw the rubbish to R.)

MRS C. And you see, it's perfectly all right.

(The rubbish comes back over them.)

MRS C. & BILLY — Oh, fooey! (They stump off R.)

(BROODY looks out from behind mast.)

BROODY — Hard-a-port and hard-a-starboard!

HELMSMAN — Hard-a-port and hard-a-starboard! (Jerks wheel both ways.)

(ROGER and RUPERT stagger L. then R.)

ROGER — It's his fault! After him!

(BROODY runs laughing off U.R. chased by ROGER and RUPERT as SUKEY runs on L.)

SUKEY — Broody, where are you? (She goes to look behind mast.)

(WILL enters R.)

WILL — Helmsman, this ship's spinning like a cork. Lash the wheel and go off watch.

HELMSMAN — Aye, aye sir. (He puts a rope round wheel and exits.)

WILL — It's nearly brought on one of my giddy spells. And what's all this rubbish?

(ROGER and RUPERT return L., panting.)

RUPERT — It's not fair, flying up to the crow's nest.

WILL — I didn't mean you to empty the swill buckets on the deck!

ROGER — We didn't, you see -

(<u>EFFECT 4. Seven bells sounds.</u>)

WILL — Listen, seven bells! Clear it away! We've got a mutiny in half an hour.

(ROGER and RUPERT gather up the rubbish into buckets.)

SUKEY — (looking out from behind mast) A mutiny! (She disappears again.)

WILL — Don't squeak at me. You know perfectly well we're mutinying here at eight bells, so hurry up and tidy the deck. I want this to be a clean fight. (Exits R.)

ROGER & RUPERT Aye, aye, sir. (They exit L., loaded with buckets and the deck chairs.)

SUKEY (emerging) A mutiny! I must do something, find somebody. Billy! Polly! Robinson! Anybody! (She runs off L.)

(POLLY enters R.)

POLLY Everybody's busy about the ship, but I can't get anyone to give me a job. In a house I could walk round with a duster and at least look as if I was doing something, but you can't look as if you're dusting a ship. And there aren't any flowers to arrange or - wait a moment there's that one; it's practically an arrangement in itself. I'll brighten up the Captain's cabin with it as a surprise for Robin. (She moves towards sunflower.)

(AUDIENCE shout. ROBINSON enters R.)

ROBINSON Well, well - you can't trust anybody.

POLLY Robin! I was going to surprise you.

ROBINSON I seem to have surprised you instead.

POLLY I was going to use this to brighten up your cabin. I'm trying to make myself useful. You know, just because I'm one of the owners there doesn't seem to be anything I can do on a ship.

ROBINSON Oh, but there is. It's laid down in the naval manual - lady owners when aboard have to keep the Captain happy.

POLLY I'm not sure I believe that.

ROBINSON Then let's start an old naval custom - because you do it awfully well, just by being here.

<u>MUSIC 22.</u> "NEARBY"

Please stay quite nearby.
I hope you will stay fairly near to me,
Near enough to know a strange intoxication.

POLLY Please stay quite nearby.
I hope you won't go very far away -
Near enough for me to feel your heart a-beating.

ROBINSON I could not ask that you come closer than this -

POLLY

No closer than two people in love can be when they kiss.

BOTH

I know I might die
If ever you were not nearby to me,
Near enough for me to reach out with my hand.
From now till the end of my days,
And know you're always there.
Please stay nearby for ever.

(They exit L. SUKEY enters R.)

SUKEY

Oh, where is everybody? It'll be eight bells any minute now. Polly! Billy! Sukey! Oh no, that's me. Well, if I'm the only one that's here, it'll have to be me.

(BILLY enters R. and POLLY L. as SUKEY strikes a dramatic pose.)

Alone and unaided I'll save the ship. When terror strikes only I will be prepared, only I can quell the mutinous crew. Gosh, I'm brave!

BILLY & POLLY

(applauding) Here here! Bravo! Encore! etc.

SUKEY

Billy! Polly! Thank goodness. Listen, do you know there are pirates aboard? I heard two of them plotting by a yard arm.

BILLY

You mean there are pirates at the bottom of our yard arm?

SUKEY

I mean that when the crew assemble for their tot of rum at eight bells -

(EFFECT 5. Eight bells begins to sound off.)

Quick, to the armoury! This way!

(They run off R. MUSIC 23. WILL enters L. carrying a cutlass. ROGER and RUPERT enter stealthily backwards L. and bump into him.)

WILL

Aah! Oh, it's you. You're ruining my nervous system. Now, when I tackle Crusoe, you hold the rest of them at bay. Ready?

ROGER

(feeling in his pockets) Er - not quite. You know you said to conceal our arms about us. Well -

RUPERT (feeling in his pockets) Ah! (Brings out a pencil.) Oh, a pencil.

WILL Splendid, you can write them a threatening note. A pencil!

RUPERT Well, it's a propelling pencil. I could fill them full of lead.

WILL Doh! Here he comes!

(CHORUS begin to assemble from either side.)

Do something!

(ROBINSON enters L. CHORUS all salute him while ROGER and RUPERT take off their hats to scratch their heads in puzzlement and find small pistols balanced on them.)

ROGER & RUPERT Of course!

ROBINSON Right, lads, time for your tot of rum. Bo'sun!

(As one of the CHORUS is about to step forward, WILL advances on ROBINSON, cutlass poised and ROGER and RUPERT move towards the CHORUS pistols at the ready.)

WILL Stay where you are! If anyone moves they're as good as dead.

ROBINSON What's the meaning of this, Mr Atkins?

WILL Mutiny's the meaning, Mr Crusoe. I'm taking over this ship! (He forces ROBINSON to back round so that he is standing with his back to the exit D.L., his hands behind his back.) And you, Mr Crusoe, are going to walk the plank. But first - hand over your treasure map.

CHORUS Treasure!

WILL Aye, lads, this ship's on a treasure voyage and if you stand by me you'll all get your share. Well, Mr Crusoe, anything to say?

(POLLY looks on cautiously D.L. and slips a cutlass into ROBINSON's hands.)

ROBINSON Yes, Mr Atkins. (Brings the cutlass round.) This is my answer!

(MUSIC 24. A fight ensues during which BILLY enters D.R. and stands also with his hands behind his back. WILL is disarmed at the end of the fight.)

WILL Curses!

ROBINSON Disarm those men!

(SUKEY has appeared behind BILLY and put in his hands a small keg of gunpowder with a fizzling fuse. ROGER and RUPERT throw down their pistols.)

BILLY Leave it to me! Drop those - Oh, you have.

(SAILORS seize ROGER and RUPERT and POLLY runs up from hatchway to ROBINSON and SUKEY runs on to BILLY)

POLLY Robin, are you all right?

ROBINSON Yes, my love, thanks to you.

SUKEY Billy, are you all right?

BILLY No, my love, thanks to you.

MRS C. (running on R.) Am I missing something?

BILLY (standing with shaking knees-wood-block knocks from Drummer) We'll all be missing something in a minute.

MRS C. (taking it) Why, what is it?

BILLY Gunpowder!

MRS C. Aah! (She nearly drops it.)

WILL No, no! Not my - no, no! (Ignoring ROBINSON he rushes and wrenches the keg from MRS CRUSOE and pulls out the fuse.)

ROBINSON For that I'll spare your life, Will Atkins, but you must be kept under lock and key. Master at Arms, take these men below.

1 of CHORUS Aye, aye, sir.

(He and two other SAILORS take ROGER and RUPERT and WILL off R.)

ROBINSON And now -

(BROODY enters R.)

BROODY Splice the mainbrace!

ROBINSON Well said, Broody - we'll splice the mainbrace!

CHORUS Hurray!

MRS C. Well, if you say so, dear. (Picks up WILL's cutlass and is about to hack at one of the mainmast stays.)

ROBINSON Stop, mother! To splice the mainbrace is to have a double tot of rum.

MRS C. Ah, now you're talking.

ROBINSON Carry on Bo'sun, broach the cask.

BO'SUN Aye, aye, sir!

(As the BO'SUN moves to the rum cask there is a FLASH, BLACKOUT, LIGHTS UP and DAVY JONES stands in the cask, reeling a little, to the surprise and consternation of all.)

MRS C. Ow! Bilgepipe nasty's in the rum!

DAVY Oh, no I ain't, that's in my tum.
Hic! pardon me.

ROBINSON Get off my ship!

DAVY Ay, that I will, my fine young rip,
And so will you and all beside.
Come sea! Come storm! Come wavel tide!
No tidal wave. Let gale winds whine!
And sink this ship beneath the brine!

(MUSIC 25. LIGHTNING FLASHES. Race clouds across cyc. EFFECT 6. Wind noises and thunder rolls. The crew run hither and thither with shouts and cries, DAVY gives wild shouts of laughter. Whatever scenic effects can be achieved should be used, such as loosing the mast stays from the bulwarks, slackening the lines on the mast to let it slope backwards and dropping in the sail border on one side.)

ROBINSON Abandon ship! Abandon ship!

(BLACKOUT. Fly in Scene 4 backing and half-cloth.)

Scene 4 All Adrift

This is mainly a U.V. sequence and requires a dark, unobtrusive backing. Set below it is the black half-cloth referred to at the end of the last scene. This could be a border, but flown in till its bottom edge rests on the stage. It should be 3 ft 6 ins deep with a ripple of fluorescent paint or material along its top edge to represent a line of waves. Until it is flown out all entrances and exits should be made above it unless otherwise indicated. There are notes on the cut-outs used in this scene in the Prop Plot: the CHORUS in dark clothing can operate those not worked by the PRINCIPALS.

MUSIC 25 continues, backed by hurricane force wind noises. A cut-out of "The Venturer" appears L. and pursues a much wave-tossed, wind-buffeted course to R., where it is quite overcome by the storm and sinks.

DAVY JONES enters L., apparently seated in the rum cask, with his legs from the knees down hanging over the side. He spins round and round to C., obviously very pleased with events and still very merry. BRITANNIA enters R., apparently seated side-saddle on a dolphin. She is much exasperated and tries to quell the storm. DAVY is amused by her failure so to do and cocks a snook at her. Enraged by this she jabs at his cask with her trident and evidently causes it to spring a leak for he sinks out of sight. She does not enjoy her triumph long for as she rides past the spot where he sank his trident comes up and prods her dolphin's tail and it bolts off L. with her.

The wind dies away.

SUKEY swims on L. with BILLY. They are back to back in a lifebelt clearly inscribed "The Venturer". SUKEY propels them forward with a few strokes then rests. BILLY strikes out in the direction he is facing and takes them back almost as far as they had proceeded. BILLY rests and SUKEY takes them to R. again, but as before when she rests BILLY's efforts take them back again. SUKEY makes a more determined effort, but so does BILLY and they don't move at all. Suddenly he starts to back paddle like mad. SUKEY looks round to see why as a cut-out of a saw-fish swims on L. SUKEY splashes out frenziedly and they bolt off R. as fast as they can with the sawfish following.

A small raft appears L. ROGER and WILL are seated on it lazily paddling. RUPERT is propelling it, apparently in the water. A large crab comes up and nips him. (This requires a partial costume made so that the wearer's arms operate the pincer claws.) RUPERT swims faster, ROGER and WILL paddle furiously and all exit R.

A small cut-out of a sea horse enters L. and proceeds R. It is followed by a larger one. Just as the second one exits R. a third, still larger sea horse enters L. with MRS CRUSOE riding on it, apparently trying to restrain her mount until she sees the reason for its attempted haste - a cut-out of the dorsal fin of a shark which has entered behind her. She whips up her mount like a jockey and streaks off R. The fin follows in pursuit.

DAVY JONES, minus his rum cask, has entered keeping himself out of sight and now rises slowly R.C. to stand as if conducting the elements with his trident and the music becomes more stormy. POLLY swims on L., obviously exhausted. She sinks, then rises to make another feeble stroke or two before sinking once more just as ROBINSON enters L., clinging to a spar of wood. As POLLY rises a second time he strikes out energetically towards her and reaches her just as she is about to sink again and pulls her onto the spar. DAVY has been watching this and now suddenly points his trident at them. There is a sting in the music and the spar breaks in two. DAVY wafts his trident and POLLY is carried swiftly away on her half to exit R. ROBINSON tries to follow, but DAVY holds his trident upraised against him and thrash about as he will ROBINSON can make no progress. DAVY makes another gesture and ROBINSON is lifted off the spar as if a great wave has struck him. The spar whirls round and round on its own, worked by an operator who has come on below the half-cloth. DAVY points downwards and despite his struggles ROBINSON sinks. DAVY, filled with delight and triumph, follows after him.

The half-cloth is raised slowly and flown out. The spar operator makes it appear to sink and disappear by concealing it before going off.

A shoal of small fish appears from L. and swims gently across to exit R. as two large starfish cut-outs enter there and are spun on their spindles by their operators to make them seem to cartwheel across to L. Two shrimps enter there and swim backwards to R. like jack-knives opening and shutting. As they exit R. two jellyfish enter and swim across like umbrellas opening and closing, sometimes rising in a swift diagonal and then descending in a more leisurely fashion. As they drift off L. three eels enter there. (They are three of the CHORUS with the eels delineated in fluorescent material from the tip of one outstretched arm across the body to the tip of the other.) Worked thus they perform a sinuous dance and exit R. A huge octopus cut-out enters R., operated by two persons who have fluorescent material down their legs to represent four of the creature's tentacles. Padded sticks similarly treated represent the other four. The octopus enters sideways to C. where it suddenly breaks into a Tiller Girl routine, kicking up and twirling alternate tentacles. It continues across stage like this and exits R. with a flip of its extreme L. tentacle.

Fade U.V. LIGHT. If feasible, bring up RIPPLE PROJECTOR, which continues to play until the transformation in the next scene. DAVY JONES enters L. He has a large key on his belt.

<u>MUSIC 26.</u> "DOWN BELOW"

DAVY

O life on the ocean wave
Is fine, say those who know;
But I add with haste that for my taste
It's better here below.
The rain up there can chill yer,
The icy wind can kill yer;
But here we're not familiar with such awful stuff as snow.
Ha ha ha ha ha ha ha ha, ho ho ho ho ho!

Our spirits are never damp;
Time has no ebb and flow.
Our life is light through darkest night

With phosphorescent glow.
Our mermaids are most dishy;
And though that might sound fishy,
That's just our kind of cliché in our kingdom here below.
Ha ha ha ha ha ha ha ha, ho ho ho ho ho!

(Fly backing and bring up LIGHTS to reveal Scene 5.)

Scene 5 Davy Jones's Locker

Fullset, with a gauze cloth backing in front of the rostrum to begin. This cloth depicts an underwaterscape of coral groves and seaweed copses, of rotting hulks and rusty anchors buried in the sandy sea bed. There is a rock piece R. with a heavy door in it, inscribed "LOCKER" and with a rock ground row coming out from it. On the L. is a rock wing. A seashell throne stands L.C.

DAVY JONES moves back and sits on the throne.

DAVY
Welcome shipmates, to 'neath the sea.
This cosy nook that's home to me. (He laughs.)
And home to many more beside
That once upon the sea did ride.
(Pointing to Locker.)
There they sleep in a cold sea bed,
Sleeping sound the sleep of the dead.
Now there's one more to stow his gear. (Calls to L.)
Sea Guards! Bring the prisoner here.

(The male CHORUS, as SEA GUARDS, bring ROBINSON on from L.)

What ho, my hearty!

ROBINSON
Who are you?
And where am I?

DAVY
Well, as to who
I'm Davy Jones, so where's not hard –

Full fathom five once said a bard,
Though nearer fifty 'tis to here,
Much further than you'd "shake a spear",
(Guffaws heartily.)
Forgive the little jokes I try.

ROBINSON Well, hearing them, I'll gladly die.

DAVY (laughing even more)
That's what I like, a sense of fun.
Your doom lad ain't for aught you've done.
But there's one guards your ev'ry hour
And you must die to break her power.

ROBINSON I see. And all my crew as well?

DAVY (shaking head)
Safe and sound, for I cast a spell.
Why, even now on a desert isle,
North East from here a nautical mile,
That bird of yours has just touch'd down.
'Tis only you that's earn'd fate's frown,
And that fate's certain as the tide -
Guards! Sling this jolly tar inside!

(Two GUARDS open the heavy Locker door, which reveals a tasteful array of skulls and bones and a lot of gloom. Two others push a struggling ROBINSON into the doorway. DAVY gives the key from his belt to a 5th GUARD.)

No use to struggle and to strive,
No man from there's come back alive!

(The door is shut and locked on ROBINSON. The 5th GUARD returns the key to DAVY.)

And that's Britannia's power done -
The Game is mine! The battle won!
She cannot penetrate down here!

BRIT. (off R.) That's where you're very wrong, I fear!
(She flaps on from U.R. in frogman flippers and aqua-lung gear, and carrying a three-pronged harpoon gun.)
Modern science has come to my aid.
(Levels harpoon gun at DAVY.)
So, stick 'em up! This is a raid!

DAVY

You silly seacow! What a sight.
All right then, if you want a fight,
On her, Guards!

(They start to surge forward.)

BRIT.

Stay! If life you prize.
I too have aides. Sirens, arise!

(MUSIC 27. Ballet. The females of the CHORUS, as a bevy of luscious SIRENS, undulate up from behind the rock ground row where they have been concealed. In the ballet the GUARDS are all aggression and the SIRENS all feminine wiles. They turn every war-like gesture of the GUARDS into a caress until the latter are literally entranced. When DAVY tries to rally his forces the SIRENS turn their concentrated attention on him and distract his attention while one of them takes the key from him and passes it to BRITANNIA who releases ROBINSON and takes him off R. DAVY and his MEN are completely overcome and are lured off L. by the SIRENS. MUSIC 28. FADE RIPPLE PROJECTOR. LIGHTS UP behind gauze, FADE D.S. LIGHTS and fly gauze slowly. The peak of a desert island hillock topped by a palm tree is revealed on the rostrum. ROBINSON staggers on from R. on the rostrum and sinks exhausted at the foot of the palm tree.

CURTAIN. CURTAIN UP.

BROODY flaps on wearily from L. on rostrum to collapse beside ROBINSON. LIGHTS UP D.S. to pick out BRITANNIA in the middle of her SIRENS all pointing triumphantly at ROBINSON.

CURTAIN

MUSIC 29. ENTR'ACTE

PART II

Scene 6 Robinson Crusoe's Island

Fullset. Cut-out of lush tropical vegetation along back of rostrum. The rostrum front is covered to look like a rock formation coming through the undergrowth. Tree wing R. with gauze panel in it. On the L. is a hut piece, looking like a rough-hewn wood construction. It has several notches cut in the onstage edge. There is a window opening with a roughly made bench under it and a door, on one side of which are two coconuts and on the other a goatskin umbrella.

MUSIC 30. The scene opens in darkness. As the lights come up slowly we hear EFFECT 7, the cries of various jungle birds – a sort of jungle dawn chorus. When the lights are fully up BROODY puts his head out of the window.

BROODY (cooing) Lovely birdies! Lovely birdies!
(Angrily.) Shut up! (He withdraws his head.)

(After a short pause ROBINSON appears in doorway, now wearing a goat-skin outfit, with a knife in his belt. He yawns and stretches then picks up the coconut and clicks his tongue.)

ROBINSON That monkey's only left two coconuts again, Broody. (He puts them inside.)

(There is a subdued murmur from BROODY off.)

Don't go to sleep again, Broody. It's a lovely day. (Steps out of hut and sighs.) But then it always is here. (Cuts a notch in the side of the hut with his knife.) Lovely day after lovely day after – I suppose I shouldn't, but sometimes I long for a bit of fog, or a shower – well,

I'd settle for a couple of clouds. (Finishes the notch.) But there it is, another lovely day. (Counts a few notches.) Ah, Friday. That's good, I always expect something special to happen on Fridays. We came ashore here on a Friday and it was another Friday when the wreck of "The Venturer" was washed up in the bay. I don't know what we'd have done without the stores and weapons we brought off that.

(BROODY enters from hut looking disgruntled.)

Ah, good morning, Broody.

(BROODY gives a muttered squawk and hunches his head in his shoulders.)

(going to him and scratching his head) What's the matter? Have I got you up too early?

(BROODY nods decisively and jerks his head away.)

All right, don't speak to me, be disgruntled. But it would be much nicer if you were - what's the opposite of disgruntled? Gruntled? No, that sounds worse than disgruntled. Perhaps it depends how you say it. (Over heartily.) By jove! I'm feeling gruntled today! No, it still sounds like an angry hedgehog.

(BROODY gives a squawk of laughter.)

Ah, I made you laugh, you must speak to me now.

(BROODY tries to look as if he hadn't laughed and hunches up even more bad-temperedly. ROBINSON brings a long-muzzled gun from inside hut doorway and sits on bench to clean it with a bit of rag in the end of a ramrod.)

Well anyway, we must hunt something for breakfast, we can't laze about all day, Polly.

BROODY Not a Polly!

ROBINSON Yes, you are, you're a pretty Polly.

BROODY Asterisk!

ROBINSON What?

BROODY Asterisk! Asterisk! Asterisk! Lots of asterisks! (Runs off into hut.)

ROBINSON (laughing) Such language! Don't worry, I don't really think you're a pretty Polly. (Sighs.) No, not at all, not like my Polly.

MUSIC 31. "PRETTY POLLY" (Reprise)

(FADE STAGE LIGHTS and bring up a single SPOT on ROBINSON.)

Pretty Polly, Pretty Polly! Such a lovely name
To call her any other would be an awful shame.

(FADE UP LIGHT behind gauze panel in tree wing R. to reveal POLLY. (It will be effective if her voice can be miked and fed through an echo chamber.))

POLLY When they called me Pretty Polly I was most distressed;
But when I heard him speak it, straightway I liked it best.

BOTH What made my lonely heart rejoice
And set my love aflame?
Is there enchantment in a voice
And magic in a name?

POLLY Once he called the name of Polly -

ROBINSON Whisper it and sigh.

BOTH Then as we loved each other and all the years go by,

(FADE gauze light.)

ROBINSON I'll love the name of Polly till I die!

(Bring UP STAGE LIGHTS. BROODY re-enters from hut and rubs his head consolingly against ROBINSON.)

Thank you, Broody. Come on, then, let's find our breakfast. (He picks up and opens the goat-skin umbrella then picks up his gun.) Silly of me to think of Polly like that. After all, I'm not likely to see her again. In fact, I'm not likely to see anybody again. (He exits U.L.)

(BROODY follows with a dejected squawk. MUSIC 32. MAN FRIDAY runs on from R. breathing heavily. He sees the hut and stops abruptly, obviously surprised by it. He looks cautiously off and seems satisfied his pursuers are not in sight. He moves warily to the hut and drops on all fours to crawl under the window, then rises slowly to peer in. He moves to the door and knocks gently. He pushes the door open and jumps back lest anyone should rush out. Deciding that all is well he looks inside. Slight pause. He moves out again. The sunflower catches his eye and he moves to it with the obvious intention of picking it. The AUDIENCE shout astounds him and he turns and runs off R. ROBINSON and BROODY run on U.L.)

Goodness, I never thought to hear that here. But I can't see anybody, can you?

(BROODY shakes his head.)

(suddenly seeing something just inside hut) Wait, Broody, look! A footprint! A human footprint! A naked human footprint!

(BROODY hides his eyes.)

Then there's another man on the island!

(BROODY jumps up and down fluttering his wings then runs up onto rostrum.)

Why, there may be several. Any sign of a boat, Broody?

(BROODY gives a single urgent squawk and points a wing R.)

(running to join him) A boat - there's dozens! And all war canoes by the look of them!

(There is a cry of despair off R. followed by a whoop of exultation from several voices. MUSIC 33. A drum begins to beat, and is answered by another drum.)

Quick, Broody, we must hide! They're coming this way!

(They run off U.L. The drumming multiplies. Suddenly one of the CHORUS as a WITCH-DOCTOR CANNIBAL leaps on-stage with a blood-curdling yell. He is followed by the rest of the CHORUS as war-painted CANNIBALS dragging on FRIDAY. They fling him down and a savage dance ensues during which FRIDAY tries to break away several times. Eventually his hands are bound with a rope, the drumming grows and grows in intensity and just as the climax is reached and FRIDAY is obviously about to be slain, EFFECT 8 a shot rings out from U.L. The drumming stops dead, and the dancers freeze in terrified amazement. EFFECT 9 a second shot and the CANNIBALS run helter-skelter off R., shouting and jabbering. ROBINSON runs on from U.L. and hastens to untie FRIDAY while BROODY follows on and fans him with his wings.)

It's all right, Broody, he hasn't fainted, I think he's just frightened. I wonder if he speaks any English. A bit of pidgin, maybe.

(BROODY nods, indicates that he himself does then nudges FRIDAY and coos at him like a dove.)

No, Broody, not pigeon like a bird, pidgin English. Like this. (To FRIDAY.) You no worry. You safee. We save-um you. You savvy?

(FRIDAY stares blankly at him.)

You savvy pidgin? Me speakee pidgin - you no speakee pidgin?

(FRIDAY scratches his head.)

(to BROODY) No, I don't think he does speakee pidgin - I mean, speak pidgin. Let's see if we can find out his name, anyway. (To FRIDAY with elaborate gestures.) Me Robinson. Him Broody. You who?

BROODY Yoo-hoo!

ROBINSON Broody! Don't confuse things. As we can't find out his real name let's give him one. Any ideas?

BROODY Pretty Polly!

ROBINSON Broody! We want to give him a special sort of name. I know, I said something special happens on Fridays here and it has, we've found another man. So let's call him that - Man Friday. (To FRIDAY.) You Man Friday.

FRIDAY I am? Well, thank goodness you didn't find me on a Monday. I hate Mondays.

ROBINSON You can speak English!

FRIDAY Fluently, but you seem to have a little difficulty with it. All this save-um and speakee stuff - would you like me to teach you to speak it properly?

(BROODY goes off into squawks of laughter.)

ROBINSON Broody!

BROODY Him Friday. Me Broody. You silly! (Laughs even more.)

FRIDAY How interesting, a parrot with a sense of humour.

(BROODY is very pleased and puts his head down to be scratched which FRIDAY does.)

ROBINSON Well, you could call it that, I suppose. But what's your real name?

FRIDAY Ob-lan-gan-go-cum-hawangee-kin-ni-naga-hoo. But in England I was known as Fred. I think I prefer Man Friday, though.

ROBINSON Oh, you've been to England?

FRIDAY For most of my life. Just before I left, I was up at Oxford getting my M.A. I only came back to my island near here recently to take up the chieftanship of my tribe. That was some of my tribe you so kindly frightened off.

ROBINSON They treat their chiefs in a funny way then.

FRIDAY Well, I'd quarrelled with them about their diet. You see, with them one man's meat is another man's flesh.

ROBINSON You mean, cannibals?

FRIDAY Exactly. It creates rather a social problem.

ROBINSON A social problem?

FRIDAY Yes, everybody wants to have everybody else for dinner. For the sake of survival I suggested they took up Vegetarianism.

ROBINSON And what happened?

FRIDAY They said yes and would I taste better with peas or carrots.

ROBINSON Well, I'm glad I was here to save you.

FRIDAY Believe me, so am I. But I'm afraid it's put you in danger now. They'll be back in a day or so.

ROBINSON That's all right. I've guns and plenty of powder and shot, and two of us can fight better than one.

FRIDAY We can fight better still if I build a stockade. I'll be glad of the practical experience, too. I'm preparing a thesis on structural engineering for my Ph.D.

(BROODY gives an incredulous whistle.)

ROBINSON My sentiments exactly, Broody. Of course, if we're lucky we could be rescued by a passing ship.

FRIDAY Um, ships steer clear of these islands. The nearest they come is Trinidad.

ROBINSON If only we could get a message there. (Brings out treasure map.) I wrote an S.O.S. ages ago, but I couldn't think how to send it anywhere.

FRIDAY What's this it's written on? (Examines it.)

ROBINSON The only paper I had, a treasure map, but that's not much use when you're stuck on a desert island; not even as an S.O.S. when you haven't got a bottle or a pigeon.

BROODY Him Friday - me Broody. (Chortles.)

ROBINSON Oh, Broody, you know very well I mean a carrier pigeon. Do try to be helpful.

FRIDAY Well, he could be very helpful.

(BROODY preens himself, pleased.)

As a carrier parrot.

BROODY What!

ROBINSON Broody, that's a wonderful idea!

BROODY Nuts!

ROBINSON But think, you could be a hero - bravely flying over the sea, flying on and on and then -

BROODY Sinking.

ROBINSON Yes, maybe you're right. In fact, you probably wouldn't get airborne at all.

BROODY (giving an outraged squawk) Clever Broody! (He runs flapping his wings violently.)

ROBINSON Wait! We haven't tied on the message yet. I was only teasing, though. I knew we could rely on you really, Broody.

FRIDAY (tying the map on BROODY's leg with the rope that was round his wrists) Now Trinidad lies due South West of here.

(BROODY thinks about that and then points a wing off R. enquiringly.)

(nodding) Right on course.

ROBINSON Good-bye, Broody - and thank you.

(BROODY looks huffy, but relents and rubs his head against ROBINSON and puts it down for him to scratch.)

BROODY Bye-bye.

ROBINSON Good luck, Broody.

BROODY (moving L.) Good luck, Broody.

FRIDAY That's right, get a good run for your take-off.

(BROODY puts his head down, flaps his wings with increasing speed then runs off R. ROBINSON and FRIDAY give him a cheer and look off after him.)

ROBINSON That's it - up - up - up! Mind that PALM TREE! (Gives a sigh of relief.)

FRIDAY We have lift off.

ROBINSON Good old Broody! I hope he makes it all right.

FRIDAY If he keeps flying South West he can't miss it. By the way, do you know where this island lies?

ROBINSON No, why?

FRIDAY It's eleven degrees nine minutes North and sixty degrees twelve minutes West, give or take a second or so. I thought it might interest you.

ROBINSON In a way, yes, but I don't - wait a minute. That's the latitude and longitude of the island on my map! But without the map we don't know where the treasure's hidden.

FRIDAY Well, if we go to the other side of the island by the lagoon I don't think we'll have much trouble finding it. Naturally I noted its position before I tied the map to your parrot's leg.

ROBINSON Friday, you're a wonder.

FRIDAY Not quite that, but life's full of opportunities; I just don't believe in wasting them.

MUSIC 34. "THE WAY TO THE TOP"

Take a tip from me, I'm a connoisseur,
I will make us great, on my honour, sir.

BOTH As from today we're on the way to the top.

ROBINSON When a situation is tactical
I admit that you're very practical.

BOTH As from today we're on the way to the top.

FRIDAY If there is a chance go and get it -

ROBINSON I'm getting it.
If there is a horse that's a winner -

FRIDAY I'm betting it.

BOTH Give us just an inch and we'll take a yard,
That is our plan
And take it we can.

FRIDAY We will reach the top in our unity.

ROBINSON We will never miss opportunity.

BOTH As from today we're on the way to the top.

(Dance.)

None of our demands is perimeted;
As a company we're unlimited.
As from today we're on the way to the top.

(BLACKOUT. Close traverse tabs and fly in Scene 7 cloth.)

Scene 7 Meanwhile, in Port of Spain

Open tabs when ready during scene to reveal a frontcloth of colourful Caribbean waterside.

ROGER and RUPERT enter R. RUPERT holds a placard on a stick which reads "JOLLY ROGER & RUEFUL RUPERT. HIRE SERVICE PIRATES".

ROGER Pirates! Hire Service Pirates! Lovely Pirates! All fresh!

RUPERT I don't know what you're going on like that for. There's nobody here.

ROGER I'm drumming up some trade, Rupert. After all, we're in the Caribbean, the world centre of piracy, so somebody's bound to want us soon; especially as we're the one and only firm of Hire Service Pirates. (Calls.) Pirates! Pirates! Hire Service Pirates!

1st PIRATE (off R.) Pirates! Pirates! Hire Service Pirates!

ROGER Funny echo here.

(As he starts to call again the same voice chimes in and ROGER's trails away. One of the MALE CHORUS as a PIRATE enters R. accompanied by another, who carries a placard on a stick which reads "SAM SKULDUGGERY & CUTTHROAT CUTHBERT. HIRE SERVICE PIRATES". They cross in front of ROGER and RUPERT to L.)

1st PIRATE Pirates! Pirates! Hire Service Pirates! (They exit L.)

RUPERT The one and only firm, eh?

ROGER Well, the two and only firms. There can't be any other –

(Two more MALE CHORUS as PIRATES enter R., one holding a placard which reads "HIGH JACK & LOW JOHN. HIRE SERVICE PIRATES". They too move across in front of the others.)

HIGH JACK (very high voice) Pirates! Pirates!

LOW JOHN (very low voice) Hire Service Pirates!

(They exit L.)

ROGER Hm, perhaps piracy is rather overcrowded in Trinidad, Rupert. Never mind, luckily we've got these to fall back on. (Produces one of his treasure maps and gives it to RUPERT.)

RUPERT Er - yes. You don't think there ought to be a bit more variety in the shape?

ROGER Ah, I've thought of that. I've brought out my Mark II version. (He brings out a map which is a perfect square with an "X" in the middle.)

RUPERT (sighing) Well, at least nobody else will be daft enough to try and sell -

(5th MALE CHORUS as a PIRATE enters R. with a placard round his neck, "GENUINE PIRATE TREASURE MAPS" and holding some samples of his work which are all triangles with "X's" in the middle. He also crosses in front of them as he speaks.)

5th PIRATE Treasure Maps! Genuine Pirate Treasure Maps! All freshly forged. Treasure Maps! (Exits L.)

RUPERT (silently handing map back to ROGER and sighing) I think I'll take up flower selling myself. I'll sell this one for a start. (Moves to sunflower.) Sunflower! Lovely fresh -

(AUDIENCE shout. He runs back and snatches the map from ROGER.)

Treasure maps!

BROODY (off L.) Thieves! Thieves!

ROGER Thieves? Now look what you've done. Quick, scarper!

(They run off R. BROODY jumps onstage from as high as possible.)

BROODY Thieves! (Looks round.) Thieves all gone. (Looks and sees sunflower is safe.) Never mind. (Gives a whistle of relief.) I made it. (Flaps wings excitedly.) Who's a clever - (Sways and staggers.) - Oo-er! Who's a tired birdie? Br-oo-dy. (Collapses on his back with his claws curled in the air and gives a snore and a whistle.)

ROGER (putting his head on R.) Is it?

RUPERT (putting his head on below ROGER's) It can't be.

ROGER It must be. There can't be two parrots that size. (Comes on stage.) Rupert, it's just what Will wants.

RUPERT (following on) What, a parrot that size?

ROGER No, to find out what's happened to Robinson Crusoe. Well, now we can. I'll get Will. You stay with that bird. Go wherever he goes, do whatever he does. (Exits L.)

RUPERT If he starts flying again it'll be tricky. Still, I'd better try and do what Roger says. (He looks at BROODY's recumbent form, shrugs, sighs and lies beside him with his feet curled in the air. BROODY keeps his eyes shut during the following sequence as he is still asleep. He suddenly jerks his head up and lets out a single squawk and drops his head again. RUPERT does the same. BROODY cycles his legs in the air making cawing noises then sits up abruptly flapping his wings, all of which RUPERT copies.)

BROODY Keep flying! Keep flying!

RUPERT (flapping his arms. In a parrot voice) Keep flying! Keep flying!

BROODY (still flapping) I'm a clever Broody!

RUPERT (flapping) I'm a clever .... Rupert!

BROODY Made it! Made it! Waah! (Sinks back on floor.)

RUPERT Made it! Made it! Waah! (Sinks back.)

ROGER (putting head on L.) Oh, Rupert, I forgot - Rupert, where are - ? (Sees him on floor.) Rupert! What are you doing?

RUPERT What he's doing, like you said.

ROGER (coming onstage) I didn't mean like - Hey! He's got some paper tied to his leg. (Removes it.)

RUPERT (rising) All right. I'll tie some to mine.

ROGER It's a treasure map. In fact, it's the treasure map, Robinson Crusoe's!

RUPERT Ooh yes. And he's written an S.O.S. on it.

BROODY (starting to sit up) S.O.S.? It's mine! It's mine!

ROGER Hullo, he's perking up. Quick, we'll take this to Will at the Pieces of Eight Tavern.

(They run off L.)

BROODY (struggling to rise) Come back! Come back! No good. Too tired. Rotten swine. (Flops back.)

(BILLY enters R. wearing a sandwich board which advertises "MRS CRUSOE'S BOARDING HOUSE – 'MON CARIBBEAN REPOS' 3 ~~2~~ ~~1~~, FISH ROW, PORT OF SPAIN.")

BILLY Boarding house! Boarding house! First Class Accommodation! Hurry, hurry, hurry! Get your lodgings before –

(EFFECT 10. A long rumbling crash starts off R. He reacts to the continuation of bumps and bangs then sighs and takes the sandwich board off.)

Oh well, I tried. (He takes out a pencil and strikes out the "3".)

(A dusty and dishevelled MRS CRUSOE enters R.)

All right, mother?

MRS C. Yes, thank you, dear. Really I don't know what it is with me and houses. They just seem to crumble around me.

(POLLY and SUKEY run on R.)

BOTH Mrs Crusoe! Mrs Crusoe!

POLLY Thank goodness you're all right.

SUKEY It's all our fault. We should never have banged out the doormats on the back wall.

MRS C. Ah well, you weren't to know, dears. I always bang them out on the empty house next door.

BILLY Well, why hasn't that fallen down?

MRS C. I don't know, I expect it's waiting for me to move in.

(There is a gurgle from BROODY.)

I beg your pardon?

BILLY Granted.

MRS C. No, I thought -

(Another gurgle.)

SUKEY It's something over there.

BILLY It looks like an old heap of feathers.

MRS C. It's Broody!

BILLY Ah, it is an old heap of feathers.

(They cluster round BROODY and help him to sit up.)

MRS C. Are you all right, dear? Speak to us, Broody. Say something.

BROODY Aw, people, always the same - "Pretty parrot. Say something".

BILLY Yes, he's all right. That's our Broody.

SUKEY But where's he come from?

POLLY And where's Robinson?

BROODY (cocking his head on one side to think a moment then whistling a few bars of "Sleepy Lagoon". Then -) Dit dit dit, dah dah dah, dit dit dit. (Sadly.) Yo ho ho and a bottle of rum.

MRS C. Ah, he's rambling.

POLLY No, I think he means something. (Hums tune.) That's Sleepy Lagoon -

SUKEY Desert Island Discs -

BILLY He's on a desert island!

(BROODY nods.)

MRS C. What was the next bit?

BROODY Dit dit dit.

POLLY Dah dah dah, dit dit dit - S.O.S.! Robinson's sent an S.O.S. and er - yo ho ho and a bottle of rum?

MRS C. He's thirsty?

SUKEY No, something to do with pirates -

POLLY Have some pirates taken it, Broody?

(BROODY nods.)

BILLY That's handy. Everybody's a pirate here. How can we find them?

BROODY Pieces of eight! Pieces of eight!

MRS C. Ah, he thinks he's in "Treasure Island".

BROODY (more insistently) Pieces of eight! Pieces of eight! Half of bitter, please. Cheers! Drinks all round. Fill the flowing bowl. Pieces of eight. Pieces of eight!

(They all look at him mystified.)

(exasperated, he la-la's "There is a tavern in the town, in the town") Pieces of eight!

ALL The Pieces of Eight Tavern!

(BROODY nods and gives a whistle to express "Whew!".)

POLLY Oh, you are a clever birdie!

BROODY I'm a brilliant birdie! (Sinks back exhausted.)

MRS C. Poor thing, let's get him home. We can use your sandwich board as a stretcher, Billy.

(ALL help to get BROODY on it.)

That's it, and then we must find out what's happening at the Pieces of Eight Tavern.

BILLY I bet it's something to do with Will Atkins. He always goes there.

SUKEY Then we'd better go there in disguise.

(MRS CRUSOE and BILLY lift the sandwich board with BROODY on it.)

MRS C. Soon have you home, Broody, and you can have a nice rest.

BILLY Yes, we'll sort you out the comfiest bricks from the rubble.

(They exit R.)

SUKEY Polly, I'm so glad for you, now you know that Robinson isn't - well, you know what I mean.

POLLY Yes, thank you, Sukey.

(SUKEY exits R.)

Yes, now I know he's not drowned, now I know I can hope to see him again one day. I can almost see him now -

<u>MUSIC 35.</u> "IF I JUST CLOSE MY EYES"

(Close traverse tabs and fly out cloth.)

If I just close my eyes,
Dream a waking dream
He will be clear to me, near to me.
If I just wait awhile
Calling with my heart
His ship he'll steer to me, dear to me.
Where are words to tell
All the hopes inside of me
For the moment I will run
Into his arms again?
I long for him, wait for him
Through the endless years.
Sigh for him, cry for him,
Laughing through my tears.
Now I can be strong
Till I see his face again,
Till within his heart
I can take my place again.
If I just close my eyes -
He's there! He's there!

(SLOW FADE to BLACKOUT. Open traverse tabs.)

Scene 8 The Pieces of Eight Tavern

Fullset. A sleazy Caribbean dive. At the back of the rostrum is a backing representing an open-work and ramshackle bamboo construction. L.C. on the front of the rostrum is a flat with an opening in it covered with a bead curtain and steps down in front of it. Wing L. and a wing R. with American saloon-type swing doors. D.L. is a table which has a bowl covered by a towel set on it and there are 3 chairs round the table.

MUSIC 36. The CHORUS as PIRATES and CARIBBEAN WENCHES are discovered in roisterous, boisterous mood drinking, laughing, and flirting. We see a hand fumbling to open the swing doors and BILLY comes tentatively into the opening. This is because he is wearing two eye patches as part of a pirate disguise, which is completed by a brightly coloured head-scarf and a large black and obviously false moustache. He also carries a placard on a stick reading "BARNACLE BILL. HIRE SERVICE PIRATE".

A girl runs giggling across in front of him chased by a PIRATE, whom BILLY bumps into.

BILLY Sorry, madam.

PIRATE (gruffly) What?

BILLY (raising an eye patch hurriedly) Oh, beg pardon - sir.

(The PIRATE continues chasing the girl.)

Maybe two eye patches is overdoing it. (Removes one and looks around.) I wonder where Will Atkins is? (As he says "I wonder" he assumes a "thinking" position, which he should assume on each subsequent occasion he says it.)

(WILL flings open the doors behind him and knocks him with them.)

Now look her- Oh.

WILL Well, sea scum?

BILLY I - er, I - er - (Points at his placard.) How are you off for Pirates?

WILL (peering closely at him) Haven't I seen you before?

BILLY What? Oh, no. You don't remember me at all. I mean - you don't remember me at all the places you go to because I don't go to them.

WILL I'm sure I've seen you before.

BILLY Not like this. I mean - I don't look like this - that is, I'm not who I look like.

WILL Oh? Who do you look like?

BILLY I don't know. I haven't seen him before either.

WILL Pshaw!

BILLY Yes, quite pshaw.

WILL Bah! (Strides away to table D.L.) Ugh! What a fug!

WENCH (A SERVING WENCH) Oh, Mr Atkins, you always say that. Well, I've got your Friars Balsam ready.

WILL There's a good little serving wench. And bring me -

(The rest of his speech is lost in a burst of laughter from some PIRATES and GIRLS.)

BILLY Sukey and Polly were going to disguise themselves as serving wenches. I wonder where they've got to?

(The swing doors open behind him and knock him. SUKEY enters stealthily backwards.)

SUKEY (sotto voce) Hurry up, Polly. (She turns to BILLY. She is disguised as a serving wench, but also has a large black moustache which is on an elastic.) Psst! It's me.

BILLY (fingering his own moustache) Are you sure? I thought it was me.

SUKEY Well, I'm disguised.

BILLY I don't think it looks quite - er - how about like this? (He pulls up her moustache to make a fringe under her mob cap.)

(WILL puts his head under the towel. The SERVING WENCH crosses in front of BILLY and SUKEY.)

WENCH Always the same. Always wants bitter lemon.

SUKEY Who wants bitter lemon?

WENCH (hooking a thumb at WILL) Ssh! You know who. (Moves off R.)

SUKEY (following off after her) Ah! I'll take it to him.

BILLY I wonder what happened to Polly?

(POLLY opens doors and knocks him. She is also disguised as a serving wench with an over-large mob cap coming down over her eyes.)

I must do my wondering somewhere else.

POLLY Psst!

BILLY Hullo, where have you been hiding?

POLLY (pulling up mob cap) Under here. Have you found out anything yet?

BILLY No, but only Will's here. No Roger and Rupert.

POLLY Well, I wonder where - ?

BILLY Wait! (He moves her away.) Carry on.

POLLY I was only going to say, I wonder where they are?

BILLY I know, but if you wonder that there, then they - That's odd, they didn't. (Moves back to look.) Well, I wonder where they've got to?

(ROGER bursts through doors knocking him.)

ROGER (very breathless) Mr Atkins! Mr Atkins!

SUKEY (returning from R. with a tankard. To BILLY and POLLY) I've got his bitter lemon.

ROGER Ah, for Mr Atkins, eh? (Takes it.) I'll take it to him. Where is he?

SUKEY Oh no, you can't take it. I was going to overhear what - I mean -

ROGER Ah, he's over here?

SUKEY No, over there, but -

ROGER So he is. (Crosses L.) And bring two more for me and my friend.

POLLY Ah! We'll take them, Sukey.

(They hurry off R.)

ROGER Mr Atkins - Ooh, I'm all out of breath.

WILL (emerging briefly) Share my towel.

ROGER Thanks. (He does.)

BILLY (sighing) I suppose I've got to. (Hunches awaiting the blow.) I wonder where Rupert is?

RUPERT (off outside doors) Somebody say Rupert?

BILLY (turning to doors) Yes, I did.

(RUPERT opens door in his face.)

You can't win.

ROGER Ah, Rupert, bring our drinks.

POLLY & SUKEY (entering with them) Here they -

RUPERT (taking drinks) Oh, very well.

POLLY & SUKEY But we were -

RUPERT (martyred, crossing to table) It's quite all right. I'm used to sacrificing myself.

(MUSIC 37.)

SUKEY Now how are we going to find out anything?

(They creep nearer the table as 1st PIRATE takes exception to his GIRL being too friendly with 2nd PIRATE. She scorns 1st PIRATE and embraces 2nd.)

WILL (emerging from towel) That's better. Any news?

ROGER Great news, Mr Atkins. Listen -

(As he leans forward on table the 1st PIRATE yanks the GIRL round, slaps her face and flings her onto table between WILL and ROGER and RUPERT. All this is done, of course, in time to the music.)

ROGER Ooh.

WILL Pay no attention. It happens all the time here. Yes?

ROGER Well, you see — (Continues to speak unheard by AUDIENCE.)

(Both PIRATES pull the GIRL away.)

POLLY & SUKEY — That's it!

SUKEY — Billy, kiss Polly.

BILLY — But I thought you were my -

SUKEY — Kiss, Polly!

(BILLY shrugs unhappily and gives POLLY a chaste peck on the cheek. SUKEY swings him round and lands him a stinging blow.)

BILLY — Hey, you told me to -

(POLLY grabs him and flings him on table.)

ROGER — And then the parrot - oh. They do it with men, too?

WILL — Whatever turns them on. What about the parrot?

(As WILL and the OTHERS continue to conspire silently POLLY and SUKEY yank BILLY to his feet again.)

POLLY — What were they saying?

BILLY — Eh? Oh, something about Broody.

SUKEY — Good. Throw us.

(Still a little baffled BILLY flings SUKEY, who lands in RUPERT's lap.)

RUPERT — And I said, (Flaps his arms.) "I'm a clever" - Oh.

(BILLY flings POLLY to land in ROGER's lap.)

ROGER — And then I found Robinson's - Oh. Er - yours, I think. (Shoves POLLY back to BILLY.)

RUPERT — (shoving SUKEY back) Yours too? Greedy.

(This apache dance idea is developed with BILLY receiving most of the punishment. At some point he leaps on the table so that the plotters have to speak through his legs. To avoid the interruptions WILL, ROGER and RUPERT rise and move R. and stop en route D.C. where the dancers again come between them and mistakenly take away one of the plotters and fling him around. There are snippets of dialogue all through the dance and the information gathered by a dancer should be briefly conveyed to the others.)

WILL Aha! The map! — Ah yes, North East — Treasure, of course — "X" marks the spot.

(At the end of the dance BILLY is in a state of collapse and POLLY and SUKEY seek to resuscitate him.)

Right, you know what to do. Off you go.

ROGER Aye, aye, sir.

(As he and RUPERT hurry to the swing doors they notice SUKEY and POLLY's ministrations.)

RUPERT I think they quite like him really.

(They exit through doors.)

WILL (tapping map gleefully before putting it away) He-he! Ha-ha! The passport to my revenge!

BILLY After all that we still don't know what he's up to.

SUKEY Perhaps your mum will be able to find out when she gets here in disguise.

POLLY Yes, but where is she?

(MUSIC 38. MRS CRUSOE thrusts aside the bead curtains and appears in the opening, disguised as a glamorous lady pirate, who is also a slight travesty of Long John Silver in that she has a crutch.)

MRS C. Aha!

WILL Jove! What a ravishing creature. Who are you?

MRS C. You've heard of Long John Silver? Well, I'm his sister, Short Joan Tin.

WILL A lady pirate, egad!

MRS C. That's right, they call me the Sexy Scourge of the Six Seas.

WILL I thought there were seven.

MRS C. Well, nobody's perfect.

WILL Will you join me in a drink?

MRS C. Certainly, if there's room for two of us in one glass. (She comes down steps.)

WILL Ha-ha! A scintillating wit. How delightful. Serving wench, bring me a bitter lemon and two straws.

(SERVING WENCH goes off L. to get them.)

Easy, Will, you're getting feverish with excitement. (Takes out a thermometer and puts it in his mouth.)

MRS C. (stopping by others) What have you found out?

SUKEY Only that Will's got the map.

MRS C. Leave the rest to me. (As she moves to WILL she plonks the crutch on their feet.)

POLLY Ow!

BILLY Ow!

SUKEY Ow!

MRS C. Sorry. (She takes out an "L" plate to hang on the crutch before proceeding.)

WILL (removing and reading thermometer) A hundred and ten! You gorgeous creature, I'm obviously mad about you.

MRS C. Already?

WILL I expect it's because you remind me of -

WENCH (plonking drink down between them) One bitter lemon and two straws.)

MRS C. What a funny thing to remind you of. But tell me, what are your plans?

(MUSIC 39.)

WILL (slipping an arm round her waist) Confidentially, I'm after buried treasure.

MRS C. (removing his hand) So I see.

WILL No, no, I mean on a desert island. My henchmen are out now looking for a ship to hijack.

PIRATE (HIGH JACK who happens to be passing with his placard) Hi, Will!

WILL Hi - Oh, go away!

MRS C. So soon? (Turns away.)

WILL No, not you, my pretty piratess. Please stay just where you are.

MRS C. (turning back and leaning on his foot with the crutch) Ah!

WILL Well - ooh! - maybe not just where you are.

MRS C. Eh? Oh. (Moves crutch.) Sorry.

WILL Thank you. As a matter of fact I was hoping to make you my third mate.

MRS C. Ah, you've been married before.

WILL Married? No, but I've got two men who are my first and second mates.

MRS C. Have you?

WILL So now I'm raising the rest of my crew.

MRS C. Oh, I see! (Aside.) Couldn't be better. (To WILL.) Yes, we'd love to come.

WILL We?

MRS C. Well, I've got some mates too. (Motions to POLLY, SUKEY and BILLY.)

WILL I suppose they'll do. It depends what sort of ship we can steal.

(ROGER and RUPERT hurry in through swing doors.)

ROGER Mr Atkins! A merchant brig called "The Hopeful" has just docked.

WILL Splendid! But for a brig I'll need more hands. Any more volunteers?

PIRATES Aye, aye, sir!

WILL Good lads. But there's no point in boarding her before the next tide, so what about a song from you wenches?

MUSIC 40. "CALYPSO"

POL., SUKEY & CH. GIRLS
Caribbean people's song,
Sing it loudly all day long.
When we feel we must let go
We sing a Calypso.

POLLY & SUKEY
Just a couple of dizzy dames,
Taking part in the local games;
That's the picture we try to paint
To make them think we're what we ain't!

ROG., RUP. & CH. BOYS
Caribbean people's song, etc.

ROGER & RUPERT
(trying to dance to the rhythm and failing)
We would like to be sharing with 'em
This indigenous sort of rhythm.
But the moment we take the floor
We find we simply can't count four!

BILLY & CH.
Caribbean people's song, etc.

BILLY
Here beneath the tropic sun
Are all the characters from Act One.
Life can never be really dull
If you are anywhere but Hull!

ALL
Caribbean people's song, etc.

WILL
Trinidad is just the spot
To operate when the scent is hot.
I'll allot them not a jot
Of what a lot of plot I've got!

ALL
Caribbean people's song, etc.

MRS C.
I must try to sort out this mess,
While in disguise as a Piratess.
I'm the private eye round here,
While dressed up as a private-"ear"!

(The tempo and style hots up and with some increasingly vigorous dancing, both comic and straightforward, the number builds to an exciting finale.

BLACKOUT. Close traverse tabs and fly in Scene 9 frontcloth.)

Scene 9 A Sleepy Lagoon

As soon as ready during scene open tabs to show a frontcloth of an island lagoon.

ROBINSON and MAN FRIDAY enter R. carrying a battered old wooden chest. ROBINSON also has his gun and FRIDAY a spear.

ROBINSON Well, this is the last treasure chest. What will you do with your share, Friday? It must be quite a fortune.

FRIDAY I'll make another fortune manufacturing lightweight aluminium treasure chests.

ROBINSON Oh, this one's not too bad; I can manage it back to the stockade. You do a bit of spear fishing in the lagoon and catch us something tasty.

FRIDAY Sometimes you have even better ideas than I do.

ROBINSON (laughing) Don't be too long.

FRIDAY Oh no, I won't attempt to enjoy myself. I'll just suffer it as a duty.

(ROBINSON laughs again and exits L.)

The only thing is the sun's too hot. I should have brought the umbrella. (Looks at sunflower.) I wonder - well, it's worth a try, he won't want to come running back with that heavy chest he's got - if you see what I mean. (He moves towards the sunflower.)

(AUDIENCE shout and MRS CRUSOE runs on R. She carries a very small portable record player.)

MRS C. Aah!

(FRIDAY whirls round with spear upraised.)

Ooh!

FRIDAY (smiling, lowering spear and stepping towards her) Mrs Crusoe, I presume.

MRS C. (eyeing the spear nervously) What? Yes. Yes, I am,

but I'm very indigestible.

FRIDAY Oh please, this is for spear fishing. Even my tribe wouldn't think of eating the mother of the man who saved one's life.

MRS C. What? You mean Robinson? And he's not - I mean, you haven't - ? Oh, I'm all of a confuselement. How did you recognise me?

FRIDAY From a locket Robinson showed me with two portraits in it. One's a very pretty lady -

MRS C. (patting her hair, pleased) Oh, really? Yes, well -

FRIDAY And the other's a very good likeness of you. Anyway, I'm Man Friday, or so your son calls me.

MRS C. How do you do? (She makes to shake hands with him and inadvertently grabs the end of his spear.) Ow!

FRIDAY Come with me, I'll take you to him.

MRS C. Oh, yes! No, wait. I must find the others.

(FRIDAY looks at her enquiringly.)

Well, they're called Polly, Sukey and Billy. We came here on a pirate ship because Broody brought us a message -

FRIDAY Ah, he made it to Trinidad? Good old Broody.

MRS C. Yes, and good old Broody's up in the crow's nest waiting to fly and warn us when the pirates wake up. We slipped away while they were asleep. But now I've gone and lost them.

FRIDAY They can't be far away. If we shout and make enough noise they should hear us.

MRS C. Noise? Ah, then what about my record player?

FRIDAY Your record player?

MRS C. Yes, as this is a desert island I came properly prepared. All we need is a nice loud desert island disc.

FRIDAY But we haven't any discs.

MRS C. What? Do you mean Roy Plomley's been deceiving me all these years? No discs? Not even a little one?

FRIDAY No, not even a little one.

(A huge gramophone record rolls on L. It is operated by a person behind it holding the spindle on which it rotates.)

Well, what do you know? A record record.

MRS C. There, I knew Roy wouldn't let me down - (She looks between her little player and the record.) But er, well, how are we going to play it?

FRIDAY Um - run round and round it with a needle?

MRS C. You are sharp. (Looks at record label.) "Hush-A-Bye-Baby"? That's a bit quiet.

FRIDAY We could try the flip side.

(They manoeuvre it round at the side of the stage so that the operator can slip off stage, and on again when it has been turned, without being seen. The flip side reveals the words of the Song Sheet printed round the disc.)

MRS C. Do you think it's trying to tell us something?

FRIDAY Let's sing it and find out.

MUSIC 41. "RAH! RAH! RAH!"

BOTH
I am getting very lonely
Wond'ring where the others are.
If I holler will they hear me?
Well, let's try it - RAH! RAH! RAH!

MRS C. Well, if we could sing it about five hundred times louder the others might hear us but where could we find another five hundred voices? (Or whatever is the capacity of the auditorium.)

FRIDAY I'll tell you a secret. This desert island isn't really deserted. There's a tribe of exactly five hundred people right there. (Points at AUDIENCE.)

MRS C. You do surprise me. But do you think they'd help? I mean, they're not too savage?

FRIDAY Only if you don't let them sing.

MRS C. Then, let's move the disc in the middle where they can all see it.

(Disc starts to roll R.)

Oh, how obliging.

(It stops in C. with the words upside down.)

Er - yes. (Shrugs.) Well, if you'll all just stand on your heads -

(FRIDAY motions to her to wait. The operator lifts the disc slightly and FRIDAY spins it till the words are the right way up.)

Oh, you are clever. (To AUDIENCE.) Right, altogether now. One, two -

(They let them sing a few bars and then let them peter out.)

Perhaps they don't understand English.

FRIDAY No, I'm sure they'll do better this time. (To AUDIENCE.) Won't you? (Reaction. Bellowing.) WON'T YOU? (Reaction.) Let's go then.

(When the AUDIENCE have sung the song through, HOUSE LIGHTS UP. POLLY enters at auditorium R., SUKEY at auditorium L. and BILLY at the back of the auditorium on L.)

SUKEY Yoo-hoo!)

POLLY Mrs Crusoe!) (Together.)

BILLY Hey, mum!)

MRS C. There, they did hear you. Oh, well done. This is Man Friday, dears, he's going to take us to Robinson. He was also clever enough to find that tribe of people down there.

BILLY I think there's two tribes, mother. A full-sized tribe and a pigmy tribe.

MRS C. You silly thing, they're the full-sized lot's children. Like people, only smaller. I wonder if some of those children would be too shy to come up here and sing by themselves?

(Ad lib while MAN FRIDAY, SUKEY, POLLY and BILLY encourage the children and help them onto the stage. MRS CRUSOE generally supervises on stage getting the children to sing and divides them into two groups for a competition which almost always has to be declared a draw. SUKEY, BILLY, POLLY and FRIDAY see the children safely down while MRS CRUSOE gets the remainder of the AUDIENCE to sing. When all the children are back HOUSE LIGHTS OUT.)

Well, you've been so good I'll let you all sing it just once more, so really let yourselves go. One, two -

(After it has been sung a final time BROODY runs on R. squawking and flapping his wings agitatedly.)

BROODY Who's a silly birdie? Fell asleep! Pirates! Pirates!

OTHERS Pirates!

FRIDAY Follow me to the stockade! We'll take a short cut.

((The following directions - given from the actors' point of view - assume an auditorium with aisles at each side and transverse aisles back and front; pass doors L. and R. and exit doors L and R at the back. Naturally a different layout will require the business to be suitably adapted.) FRIDAY runs over the steps L. into the auditorium and up the aisle. HOUSE LIGHTS UP. SUKEY, POLLY, MRS CRUSOE and BROODY follow. WILL, ROGER and RUPERT enter R.)

WILL There they are! After 'em!

(As ROGER and RUPERT are about to run foward BILLY pushes the disc at them then turns and follows the others into the auditorium. ROGER and RUPERT jump aside so that the disc knocks WILL down and apparently out, then trundles off R.)

RUPERT Now he can really say he's suffering from a slipped disc.

(ROGER and RUPERT follow after BILLY. Half way up the auditorium BILLY turns into a row and both start to follow him.)

ROGER I'll get him, you get the others.

RUPERT It would be me who has to get four of 'em.

(He follows after the OTHERS who go out through the exit at the top of the aisle as soon as they reach it, while ROGER follows BILLY. At the end of the row BILLY sits on an empty seat, or somebody's lap. ROGER runs past him.)

ROGER Where is he? Where is he?

BILLY I went that way. (Points up R. aisle.)

ROGER Ah, thanks.

(As he starts to run up R. aisle FRIDAY, POLLY, SUKEY and MRS CRUSOE run in through the door at the top of the aisle.)

FRIDAY Shouldn't you be behind us?

ROGER Oh, sorry, yes. (He lets them pass.)

(BILLY joins on behind the OTHERS and all run out through the door at the bottom of the aisle. As ROGER is about to follow after BILLY, RUPERT returns through the door at the top of the L. aisle.)

RUPERT Where are they?

ROGER Over here.

RUPERT How do you get there?

ROGER You have to say excuse me to all – (Looks round.) Hey, they've gone.

(They turn and run down their respective aisles and onto stage as WILL begins to recover and sit up. HOUSE LIGHTS OUT.)

BOTH Mr Atkins! Mr Atkins!

ROGER Mr Atkins, we've lost them.

WILL You would. (Starts to rise.) Oooh! Ah! Ooh!

RUPERT What's the matter?

WILL I'm not sure yet, but I'll think of something. But we must find this stockade. Let's try this way. (Moves R., but turns to move hurriedly L.) No, don't let's try that way.

ROGER & RUPERT Why not?

(Three of CHORUS as CANNIBALS leap on stage from R.)

WILL That's why not.

(Close traverse tabs and fly frontcloth during the following which presumes a FREEZE light is being used. MUSIC 42. WILL, ROGER and RUPERT run L. with CANNIBALS in pursuit. BLACKOUT and bring up FREEZE LIGHT. They all run very hard but progress very little, which gives an effect of great speed as in an old film. The CANNIBALS appear to be gaining by moving forward slightly and the OTHERS dropping back. The leading CANNIBAL prods RUPERT's behind with his spear, causing him to give a cry and run past ROGER and WILL and off L. The CANNIBAL then prods ROGER who also gives a cry and runs off past WILL. WILL puts up a hand and ALL stop. BLACKOUT FREEZE LIGHT and BRING UP STAGE LIGHTS. WILL takes three panting breaths, the CANNIBALS do the same. WILL nods. BLACKOUT and BRING UP FREEZE LIGHT. ALL start running again. ROGER and RUPERT run on R. behind CANNIBALS, give a cry and turn and run off again. The CANNIBALS turn and run off after them. When he realises he is alone WILL turns and runs off R. also. BLACKOUT FREEZE LIGHT.)

Scene 10 The Stockade

Fullset. The setting is as in Scene 6 with the addition of a wall of stakes, about 5 ft 6 ins high, running up and down stage in C. At the upstage end it curves round in front of the rostrum to go off L. A section of the central wall opens like a gate, hinged at its upstage end, to swing open to L. There is a heavy-looking bar on the gate, the free end of which can be dropped into a catch on the downstage end of the wall. The bench has been placed against the wall just upstage of the gate.

ROBINSON enters R. with the treasure chest and goes through the gate, shutting but not barring it.

ROBINSON Phew! Maybe lightweight aluminium treasure chests would be a good idea. I wonder what's in it. (Opens lid and takes out a golden goblet.) I say, gold plate! Well, I'll christen this now. (Goes to hut.) I wonder though, is coconut milk quite the thing for a golden goblet? (Exits into hut.)

(WILL, ROGER and RUPERT enter R. all bent low peering at the ground.)

WILL — Yes, along here, lads. What a bit of luck we stumbled across Robinson's tracks. I'm sure we'll strike the stockade soon. (He walks into it with his head.)

(ROGER bumps into his behind, and RUPERT into ROGER's.)

Ow! (Rubs head.) I have struck it. I shan't be able to do my yoga on my head now. Never mind, let's see what Robinson's up to. (Tries to straighten up and grabs back in pain.) Aah! I can't get straight!

ROGER — (doing likewise) Aah! Neither can I!

RUPERT — (also doing likewise) Aah! Nor me!

WILL — What? How dare you? I work very hard at being unhealthy - you're only a couple of novices. And how can we see over the wall?

ROGER — I know, let's find a lower wall.

ROBINSON — (off L.) Delicious.

WILL — Ssh! (He cups his left ear with his left hand and places it to listen against wall.)

(ROGER cups his left ear similarly and listens at WILL's other ear and RUPERT does likewise to ROGER. ROBINSON re-enters from hut, sipping at the goblet.)

ROBINSON — Um, an unpretentious little milk, but not without a certain charm. I shall lay down several nuts. Of course, it may just taste better out of gold.

OTHERS — Gold!

ROBINSON — (putting goblet back in chest and shutting lid) Anyway, I'll put it with the rest of the treasure. (Drags chest into hut.)

OTHERS — Treasure!

WILL — He's got the treasure!

ROGER — Yes, shall we rush in and overwhelm him?

RUPERT — Like this?

ROGER Well, perhaps he'd give us a handicap.

WILL No, I'll go back to the ship and fetch the rest of the crew while you keep an eye on things here. (Crosses R.)

RUPERT But suppose those cannibals catch us and cook us?

WILL (stopping beside him) Use delaying tactics. Tell them you need a pinch of salt, a bouquet garni and three hours at mark four. I'll be back with the others long before you're done. Anyway, I don't think they will come back.

(2 CANNIBALS creep on stealthily behind them from R.)

What's far more important is how I'm to get straight again.

(1st CANNIBAL jabs his bent over rear with a spear which provides the answer.)

Waah! (Turns and sees the CANNIBALS and belts off R.)

ROGER Well, he seemed to find a pretty quick cure I wonder what it was.

RUPERT Yes, and why did he suddenly run away? (To AUDIENCE.) Eh? What's that? (AUDIENCE reaction. He clutches ROGER.) Cannibals!

ROGER Don't be silly, Rupert, they're just joking. (Reaction.) Well, I don't see any Cannibals, where are they? (Reaction.) Behind us? (To RUPERT.) I thought they'd say that. Well, let's look, just to please them.

(Both turn inwards to look upstage, the CANNIBALS move round behind them, then all turn half-way back so that ROGER and RUPERT are in profile facing each other.)

I knew it, there's nobody there. (Reaction.) All right, we'll look right round then. (He moves round to face L.)

(The 2nd CANNIBAL copies his bent over position to move round after him. RUPERT and 1st CANNIBAL do likewise to R.)

Nobody over here.

RUPERT Nobody over here.

(BOTH turn inwards, but their CANNIBALS remain static so ROGER and RUPERT come face to face with them.)

BOTH Nobody any - AAH!

(With their CANNIBALS following nose to nose ROGER and RUPERT back in a half-circle to U.R.C., where they meet bottom to bottom. As they cannot move further, but their confronting CANNIBALS continue to do so they are forced slowly upright, which causes them to give little yelps of pain. The CANNIBALS leap back a pace and raise their spears. ROGER and RUPERT turn and face each other. ROGER points downstage and he and RUPERT take a sidestep down. The CANNIBALS copy them. ROGER points upstage. He and RUPERT take a sidestep up. The CANNIBALS do likewise. ROGER points downstage, but he and RUPERT take a further sidestep up, while the CANNIBALS sidestep down, then run forward and collide, the 2nd knocking down the 1st, who obviously takes umbrage and rises glaring at the 2nd. ROGER and RUPERT shake hands and run off R., RUPERT running backwards. 1st CANNIBAL advances on the 2nd who backs away until he backs into the stockade gate, which opens and he falls into the opening. This surprises them both. They look around inside. The 2nd CANNIBAL notices the sunflower and points it out to the 1st, who motions to him to go and get it while indicating that he will stay where he is, by the gate. 2nd CANNIBAL creeps to the sunflower. AUDIENCE shout, which shocks them both. 2nd CANNIBAL hares back through the gate as POLLY and SUKEY run on from U.R. and MRS CRUSOE and BILLY from D.R.)

ALL Aha!

(CANNIBALS raise their spears.)

Ooh!

(ROBINSON has run on from the hut to the gateway a beat later than the OTHERS, who now see him.)

Robinson!

ROBINSON Polly! Sukey! Mother! Billy!

BILLY Old Uncle Tom Cobleigh and all, Old uncle -

(CANNIBALS give two blood-curdling yells and leap forward. The 1st chases POLLY and SUKEY in an anti-clockwise circle inside which the 2nd CANNIBAL chases BILLY and MRS CRUSOE clockwise. All give suitable shouts and yells.)

FRIDAY (off R.) Where are they? (Runs on.) I lost them. Where are – ?

(On seeing him the CANNIBALS stop chasing the others and both chase him round the others clustered together, until there is EFFECT 11, the sudden boom of a cannon (maroon) off R. CANNIBALS stop in terror.)

MRS C, BILLY)
POL, SUKEY) The pirates!

ROBINSON Pirates?

BILLY Yes, coming to attack the stockade!

(EFFECT 12. Another boom off R. and a cannon ball thuds on stage. CANNIBALS shriek and run off U.R.)

ROBINSON Quick, all inside!

(ALL dash inside. POLLY is first and she and ROBINSON embrace. FRIDAY is last and he shuts and bars gate.)

ROBINSON Polly!)
POLLY Robin!) (Together.)

MRS C. My boy!

ROBINSON Mother. (They hug.)

SUKEY (flinging her arms wide) Billy!

BILLY But we've been together all the time.

SUKEY I know, but it seemed too good an opportunity to miss.

BILLY Maybe you're right. Sukey! (Flings arms round her.)

FRIDAY Well, I'd shake Broody by the claw if I knew where he was.

(BROODY runs in U.R. squawking loudly chased by the CHORUS as PIRATES.)

ALL Broody!

ROBINSON (running to get on bench and look over wall) Friday, get the guns!

(FRIDAY runs into hut. WILL strides on R.)

WILL That's it, lads, grab the parrot!

(They do.)

Ah, my little bird, you shall be our hostage.

(As he tries to stroke BROODY's head, BROODY nips his finger.)

Ow! I shall get psittacosis!

ROBINSON Good old Broody! Serves you right, Will Atkins.

WILL Robinson! At last I'll have my revenge. Take that pesky fowl away and see he's well guarded.

2 PIRATES Aye, aye, Cap'n. (They drag a protesting BROODY off R.)

(FRIDAY returns with two guns, joins ROBINSON on bench and hands him one.)

ROBINSON If you harm Broody by so much as one feather you'll pay dearly. (Levels gun at WILL.)

WILL Maybe - if I haven't blown you to smithereens first! (Calls off R.) Master Gunner, prepare to fire!

ROBINSON If they're using cannon so will we. There's one I got off "The Venturer" behind the hut.

(BILLY, SUKEY and MRS CRUSOE run off D.L.)

WILL The rest of you men take cover and stand by to charge when we breech the wall.

PIRATES (drawing cutlasses and going off R.) Aye, aye, Cap'n!

ROGER (off R.) Gun ready, sir!

WILL Crusoe, surrender or I'll pound you all to Kingdom Come! - Except, of course, your dear mother who is, I trust, in a place of safety.

ROBINSON Surrender? Here's your answer, Will Atkins! (He aims gun.)

(EFFECT 13. Gunshot. Music whizz as WILL's hat is

whisked off, (by a fine line attached to it).)

WILL Aah! Right, Crusoe, you've asked for it. Master Gunner, fire!

ROBINSON Down!

(He and FRIDAY crouch. EFFECT 14. Cannon boom off R. Another cannon ball lands on stage - right beside WILL.)

WILL Look out! You're supposed to be on my side. (He exits R. indignantly.)

ROBINSON I'm worried; whatever happens they've got the advantage of Broody as a hostage.

FRIDAY Then let's get round on their flank and rescue him.

ROBINSON All right. Polly, take over this. (He thrusts his gun into POLLY's hands and exits with FRIDAY into hut.)

(POLLY eyes the gun dubiously.)

ROGER (Off R.) Heave! Heave!)
) (Together.)
BILLY (Off L.) Heave! Heave!)

(ROGER and RUPERT haul on a cannon from R., as BILLY and SUKEY haul on a similar one from L. ROGER and BILLY also bring on ramrods.)

POLLY Oh well. Is this the trigger?

(EFFECT 15. Gunshot. POLLY's gun has gone off with the barrel pointing up in the air, much to her surprise. SUKEY and RUPERT simultaneously assume they have been shot and throw themselves into dramatic poses. ROBINSON, now with a pair of pistols, and FRIDAY look back on from the hut and WILL enters R. with a small keg of gunpowder.)

SUKEY & RUPERT They got me!

ROBINSON & WILL Anyone hurt?

(Music whizz. A chicken falls from flies L.C.)

POLLY (picking it up) Er - well ...

(ROBINSON and FRIDAY laugh and disappear again.

SUKEY and RUPERT rise.)

SUKEY & RUPERT — They didn't get me.

WILL — Right, lads, reload and fire.

ROGER & RUPERT — We can't.

WILL — Why not?

RUPERT — No more cannon balls.

(WILL picks up one from the stage as MRS CRUSOE staggers on L. with a cannon ball.)

WILL — Use this again then.

WILL & MRS C. — There!

(WILL places his cannon ball in RUPERT's hands and MRS CRUSOE in SUKEY's. Both recipients let the cannon balls sink to the floor in their hands.)

WILL — Now, charge!

(PIRATES run on R., shouting and waving their cutlasses. MRS CRUSOE exits L. ROBINSON and FRIDAY look up on rostrum where they are cautiously making their way to R. ROBINSON levels his pistols and FRIDAY his gun.)

Not you lot. I'm talking about the charge in the gun.

PIRATES — Oh, sorry, Cap'n, etc. (They drift off R.)

(ROBINSON and FRIDAY continue along rostrum and off R.)

BILLY — (calling off L.) Powder monkey!

MRS C. — (returning with a small gunpowder keg) I'll powder you, you monkey. There. (She puts a pinch of gunpowder into the muzzle.)

(ROGER shakes a more plentiful measure into the other cannon.)

BILLY — I think it needs a bit more than that, mother.

MRS C. — (putting in another pinch) All right, there's two. (Puts in a third pinch.) And one for the pot.

WILL & BILLY — Load!

(RUPERT and SUKEY try to lift their cannon balls and ROGER and BILLY respectively go round to help them.)

Now, ram!

(BILLY and SUKEY ram their cannon and ROGER and RUPERT theirs with equal results - the cannon balls come out at the breech ends, one onto MRS CRUSOE's foot and one onto WILL's.)

MRS C. — Yeow!)
WILL — Yarrooch!) (Together.)

BILLY — Oops, sorry, mother.)
SUKEY — Oh, Mrs Crusoe!) (Together.)

MRS C. — It's all right, dears, but I'll just go in the hut and have hysterics for five minutes. (She limps off into hut.)

(BILLY and SUKEY join POLLY on the bench.)

WILL — You fools! I've got a nasty bunion on that foot. Why didn't you do it on the other one?

ROGER — (picking up cannon ball) Anything to oblige. (Drops it on WILL's other foot.)

WILL — Waah! You incompetent idiots! You're not safe with artillery, take the barrel off and use it as a battering ram.

(ROGER and RUPERT lift off their gun barrel.)

Right, I'll say charge.

(PIRATES start to run on.)

Not yet!

(They go again. BILLY gets down and stations himself by the gate.)

Charge!

(ROGER and RUPERT charge the gate. POLLY signals to BILLY who lifts the bar on the gate and opens it so that ROGER and RUPERT rush headlong through and off L.)

Curses!

(BILLY shuts and bars gate again. EFFECT 16. Loud crash off L. BILLY, POLLY and SUKEY look off L. ROGER and RUPERT return with the end of the barrel splayed out.)

ROGER & RUPERT — We surrender.

POL. SUKEY & BILLY — Hurray!

(There are shouts off R. then EFFECT 17, a gunshot followed by squawks from BROODY.)

ROBINSON & FRIDAY — (off R.) Run, Broody, run!

WILL — What's going on? What's happening?) (Together.)

POL. SUKEY & BILLY — They've done it! Bravo! Jolly good!)

(The PIRATES run on.)

1st PIRATE — Hostage escaped, Cap'n!

(ROBINSON, BROODY and MAN FRIDAY run on R. on rostrum as MRS CRUSOE enters from hut waving a white flag on a broom handle, and also carrying a large kettle.)

3rd PIRATE — The enemy are surrendering, Cap'n.

ALL — What?

ROBINSON — (stopping on rostrum) Mother, what are you doing?

MRS C. — (getting on to bench) Well, it's tea time, dear. I'm calling a truce. (To PIRATES.) I expect you lot would like a nice cuppa too.

PIRATES — Aye, aye, ma'am!

WILL — How kind, Leti - er - dear lady. No sugar for me, though. I'm on a diet.

ROBINSON — But, mother, you can't stop in the middle of a battle just because it's tea time.

MRS C. — I can, dear.

MUSIC 43. "POLLY PUT THE KETTLE ON"

Polly, Polly, put the kettle on.

(She gives kettle to POLLY.)

TUTTI Polly, Polly, put the kettle on.

WILL & PIRATES Put the kettle on.

ROB. & FRI. Put the kettle on.

BIL. & SU. Polly, Polly, put the kettle on.

ROG. & RUP. Polly, Polly, put the kettle on.

ROBINSON Polly -

BROODY Polly -

ROB. & FRI. Put the kettle on -

MRS C, BIL. & POLLY And we'll all have tea.

(POLLY exits into hut, leaves kettle and returns immediately. ROBINSON, FRIDAY and BROODY exit L. on rostrum; WILL and PIRATES exit R.)

SU., ROG. & RUPERT And we'll all have tea!

POLLY Sukey, take it off again -

BIL. & MRS C. Sukey, take it off again -

ROG. & RUP. Sukey, take it off again -

(SUKEY exits into hut and returns immediately with the kettle.)

ALL STOCKADE. They've all gone away!

(ROBINSON and FRIDAY with mugs, followed by BROODY enter L. through hut.)

ROB., FRI. & BROODY Polly, put the kettle on.

(POLLY exits L. into hut with kettle. WILL and PIRATES enter R. with mugs.)

WILL & PIRATES Polly, put the kettle on -

TUTTI Polly, put the kettle on.

(POLLY returns with a large teapot and 5 mugs on a tray.)

We'll all have tea!

Polly, put the kettle on,
Polly, put the kettle on,
Polly, put the kettle on,
We'll all have tea.
Polly, put the kettle on,
We'll all have tea!

MRS C. Strong, or as it comes? (She starts to pour.)

(FLASH. BLACKOUT. LIGHTS UP and DAVY JONES is U.C. on rostrum. General consternation.)

DAVY You lot of lubbers, drinking tea!
What sort of sailor men are ye?
Come, lads, there's fighting to be done,
And with my help your battle's won!

WILL He's right, men. Aye, we've been too soft,
Let victory not tea be quaffed.
(Doing his Olivier.)
Lift up your spirits and in rousing tones
Cry cheers for Atkins and for Davy Jones!

PIRATES No, that we'll not! (They throw down their cutlasses.)

WILL Why this to do?

1st & 2nd We're pirates, yes -

3rd & 4th But sailors too.

5th PIRATE To fight for him's the devil's luck.

PIRATES With Davy Jones we'll have no truck.

WILL What, sea scum? What bilgepipe leavings?
You, squid's ink! You sea squirt's heavings!
Beg pardon, Mrs Crusoe dear,
I trust my words you cannot hear.

DAVY Don't worry, Will, leave this to me.
I'll raise up such a mighty sea
'Twill sink this isle and all hereon.
Ye ocean gales I call upon
From Sou Sou West to Nor Nor East,

Come rise up like some wrathful beast
And strike this isle with tempest riot!

(ALL cower back, but nothing happens. DAVY looks round distraught.)

MRS C. Well, I never, hasn't it gone quiet?

DAVY (in a desperate whisper)
Blow, blow, ye winds! (Louder.)
Rage, rage, ye gales!
(Bellowing.)
Can you not hear?

(MUSIC 44. BRITANNIA enters U.R. on rostrum.)

BRIT. Your power fails.
You'd naught on land, now from the sea
Your might shall ever banish'd be.
(She waves her trident over DAVY.)

(With a despairing howl DAVY rushes off L.)

ALL Hurray!

BRIT. (moving D.C.) Please, I but did my duty,
To win my charge love, wealth and beauty,

(POLLY and ROBINSON embrace.)

Than which there is no prize that's higher.
Others too I'll grant their heart's desire,
Such as dear Sukey to her Billy.

(They embrace.)

Even Letitia to naughty Willy.

(WILL kneels humbly to MRS CRUSOE.)

But 'ere I go, one last good deed -
Clever Broody deserves a feed.

(She waves her trident at sunflower which shoots out seeds. BROODY rushes to them squawking happily.)

And now, the good ship "Hopeful's" in the bay,
So all aboard for England.

ALL Hip hurray!

(BRITANNIA exits R.)

MUSIC 45. "LET'S GO HOME NOW"

Let's go home now. We've been gone a long,
long time,
And there's nothing now to keep us on this shore.
Though the plot was quite involved,
Ev'ry riddle has been solved.
And now we want to go back home once more.

(BLACKOUT. Close traverse tabs, fly in Scene 11 frontcloth if used.)

Scene 11 Pax Britannica

Tabs or a frontcloth which strikes a patriotic note. If a cloth is used open tabs as soon as ready during scene.

MUSIC 46. LIGHTS UP and we see a triumphant BRITANNIA R.C., much as she is depicted on a coin. That is, seated in profile with her trident upheld in her L. hand and her Union Jack-emblazoned shield beside her on her R. However, she pushes the shield which rotates and as she is moved forward we realise she is seated on a wheel-stool, as it were.

BRIT. Look what I've got for what I've done.
A prize most useful to have won,
Since guarding Britain's shore and fleet
Gets very tiring on the feet.
The only trouble's where to park it,
I shop in such a common market.
Still I'm promoted, in a sense,
That is, from one to fifty pence.
(She produces a champagne bottle from the upstage side of her wheel-stool.)
To celebrate I'll have a dram
Of this Realpagne - well, why drink sham?
(Struggles with cork.)

Just listen when I get this free,
It makes a lovely pop.

(As she removes cork, very small FLASH. BLACKOUT. LIGHTS UP and a very dejected DAVY JONES has entered L.)

DAVY (miserably) Whoopee.

BRIT. Oh, really, Jones! You've spoilt my pop.
(Turns bottle upside down.)
And also drunk up every drop.

DAVY (nodding sorrowfully and sighing)
I thought as how 'twould give me zest,
But it's just made me more depress'd.
For since you won your victory
I've got no power on land or sea;
No place to go, no place to stay,
I hide in rock pools all the day.
And yesterday I lost a tussle
Against a winkle and a mussel.

BRIT. It seems a shame to waste your talents,
So I'll in part restore the balance.
(She rises magisterially and gestures at the wheel stool with her trident and it is pulled off R. on a line.)
I'll rule supreme the upper quarter,
With you my vassal underwater.
For really, Jones, I must confess
I quite enjoy a bit of stress,
And so a friendly fight or two
I might allow. How's that with you?

DAVY Done! Tell you what, in future duels
You rule the waves, I'll waive the rules!

<u>MUSIC 47.</u> "RULE BRITANNIA"

(Close traverse tabs and fly out cloth during number.)

BRIT. When Britain first at Heav'n's command,
Arose from out the azure main,
Arose, arose, arose -

DAVY (proffering a prop rose) A rose?

BRIT. (snatching rose and throwing it off)
From out the azure main,
This was the charter, the charter of the land,
And Guardian Angels sang this strain -

Rule, Britannia!

DAVY This is a boring song.

BRIT. Jones, I have up with you put for far too long.

DAVY If only I could have my way
Your fork would be for making toast.
Your fork, your fork, your fork would be for making toast.

BRIT. Don't be ridic'lous, with my fork you can't play.

DAVY I'm the cause of all your woe and I don't boast.

Up, Britannia!

BRIT. My masterpiece you've messed.
You're a naughty little sea dog.

DAVY You're a pest.

BOTH A compromise there'll have to be,
Our enmity we'll have to cease,

BRIT. Our en -

DAVY (saluting) R.N.?

BOTH Our enmity we'll have to cease,
Thus from this moment we'll sing in harmony,
And be the best of enemies.

Rule, Britannia! And all that sort of stuff,
One more time I think will be enough.

Rule, Britannia! We sing it one last time,
And we'll only fight again in pantomime!

(They exit R. and L. Open traverse tabs to reveal Scene 12.)

Scene 12 The Wedding Feast Aboard the Good Ship "Hopeful"

Fullset. (The Scene 3 set can be used again with different facings.) The cyc. is lit to represent a night sky, pricked with twinkling starlight if possible. There are ships' lanterns lit on the stern. There are steps down as companion-ways L.C. and R.C.

MUSIC 48. CHORUS as SAILORS enter in pairs, one from each side on the rostrum and move down the companion-ways to take their bows D.C. and then move back to form diagonal lines L. and R. The PRINCIPALS follow a similar procedure forming diagonal lines in front of them. DAVY JONES enters from L. and backs to L., and BRITANNIA from R., backing R.: ROGER and RUPERT from L. and R. respectively, both backing L.: BROODY from R.C., backing R.: MAN FRIDAY from L., backing L.: BILLY and SUKEY from R. and L. respectively, both backing R.: WILL ATKINS from L., backing L.: MRS CRUSOE from R., backing R. When she has taken her bow and backed to R. the music stops and all turn to face upstage. The SAILOR at the U.S. end of each diagonal takes a pace forward and raises a bo'sun's pipe to pipe aboard ROBINSON who enters from R. on rostrum and POLLY from L.

ALL Hurray!

(ROBINSON and POLLY move D.C. to take their bow then the PRINCIPALS come in line with them and the CHORUS move upstage onto the rostrum.)

ROBINSON Our good ship "Hopeful's" homeward bound -

POLLY And happiness all hands have found.

MRS C. Of course we hope that you have too so
We get in one last rhyme to Crusoe!

FRIDAY Though really it would be more tidy
To think up words that rhyme with Friday.

BRIT. Well, now these feeble rhymes we'll halt
Though truth to tell they weren't our fault.

(Confidentially.)
The author's not our friend, you know;
In fact, the author is De-foe!

ROBINSON — To follow that I fear were surely folly,
And so goodnight from me and -

BROODY — Pretty Polly!

<u>MUSIC 49.</u> "GRAND FINALE"

TUTTI — Let's go home now. We've been here a long long time,
And our meeting has been happiness and light.
Though the plot was quite involved
Ev'ry riddle has been solved,
And now it's only left to say "Goodnight".

CURTAIN

Set throughout:

Large flower pot in front of false prosc., L., with sunflower to grow out of it on a line. The flower is secured with a second line 2 ft down the stalk to allow it to droop in Scene 2. In the centre of the flower head a flap of material covers a hole into which, during the interval, the end of a length of hose pipe is fitted. The hose is fed through a hole in the false prosc., so that dried peas can be blown down it when the seeds shoot out in Scene 10.

PART I

Scene 1

Set onstage

On housepiece R. on the door, which is held in place manually, a knocker held by a loose nail to allow it to be pulled off easily; a door knob, which should be a rubber ball, and is held similarly by a loose nail, pulled out on the offstage side to let it drop.

L. of door is an old-fashioned bell pull with a long line of wire attached to it.

Over the door is a porch canopy, one end of which is retained by a dowelling pin to be pulled out from the offstage side.

Above the canopy is a nameplate inscribed "MON SEAVIEW REPOS" retained by dowelling pins on either side.

On board above window are five stars; four of them are held by nails which can be pulled out on the offstage side, the fifth is on a short line which only allows it to fall a short distance.

Under the window is a sill with flower pots on it. The sill is retained by a dowelling pin on one end to be pulled out from the offstage side.

On either side of the window are shutters also retained by removable dowelling pins.

On the roof is a chimney pot. It is set on a small ledge protruding to the offstage side and is pushed off the ledge with a bamboo cane to make it fall.

Off R.

Child's scooter. On handlebars are a hooter and a shopping bag containing a scraggy chicken.	MRS CRUSOE
Map of treasure island and a bag containing sunflower seeds.	ROBINSON
Throat spray, bottle of pills and a flask of gin.	WILL ATKINS
Bass broom.	MRS CRUSOE
Cut-out of a child's paddle boat, numbered "4" fore and aft. On its reverse side there is a handle for ROGER's L. hand and a strut at right angles to the cut out for RUPERT's L. hand. There is a hole in the C. of the strut.	ROGER & RUPERT
Cutlass with stiff little skull and crossbones flag jutting out at the top of the blade.	ROGER
Large bag with treasure maps, which are headed "GENUINE PIRATE TREASURE MAP", below which is a perfect circle with an "X" in the middle of it.	ROGER
Scroll of paper and a quill pen.	BILLY
Huge packet of "KWELLS".	MRS CRUSOE

Off L.

Pile of ledgers.	BILLY
Piece of paper.	SUKEY
Large smelling salts bottle.	WILL ATKINS

Personal

BRITANNIA	Trident.
DAVY JONES	Trident.
ROGER	Pop-gun.
RUPERT	Pop-gun.

Scene 2

Off L.

Large bottle labelled "WHIFFINURE"	MRS CRUSOE

Scene 3

Set onstage

Piece of rope by ship's wheel.

Off R.

2 deck chairs.	BILLY & MRS CRUSOE
Rubbish.	To be thrown on (2 cues).
Keg of gunpowder with fizzling fuse.	SUKEY

Off L.

Long leash.	BROODY
4 wooden buckets filled with rubbish.	ROGER & RUPERT
Rubbish.	To be thrown on.
Cutlass.	WILL ATKINS
Propelling pencil.	RUPERT
Small pistols.	ROGER & RUPERT
Cutlass.	POLLY

Scene 4

(All cut-outs in this scene need to be painted with fluorescent paint.)

Off R.

Cut-out of Dolphin, (fluorescent material similar to that of BRITANNIA's dress is draped over the downstage side of the cut-out to give the impression of her being seated side-saddle).	BRITANNIA
2 Starfish cut-outs, (on spindles).	2 of CHORUS
2 Jellyfish, (bell shaped umbrellas suitably painted with 4 streamers of fluorescent material hanging down for tentacles).	2 of CHORUS
Octopus cut-out and 4 padded and painted sticks for 4 of the tentacles.	2 of CHORUS

Off L.

Cut-out of "The Venturer", about 3 ft long.	1 of CHORUS
Rum cask, (covered and painted framework attached to DAVY under his arm pits. False	

legs dangle over the side to simulate the idea of his squatting in the cask).	DAVY JONES
Lifebelt, inscribed "THE VENTURER".	SUKEY & BILLY
Cut-out of Saw-fish.	1 of CHORUS
Raft and 2 paddles, (this is a platform 3 ft 8 ins high on a wheeled frame).	WILL, ROGER & RUPERT
Small cut-out of a sea horse.	1 of CHORUS
Larger cut-out of a sea horse.	1 of CHORUS
Still larger sea horse cut-out with reins and a dummy leg hanging down on the side in view to simulate the effect of MRS CRUSOE sitting astride it.	MRS CRUSOE
Cut-out of shark's dorsal fin.	1 of CHORUS
Spar of wood, (made in two halves),	ROBINSON
Shoal of fish (cut-out fishes suspended like mobiles from 2 "T" shaped black painted handles).	2 of CHORUS
2 Shrimp cut-outs, (tail half hinged to body).	2 of CHORUS
Large key to hang from his belt.	DAVY JONES

Scene 5

Off R.

Eye shield, aqualung cylinders, frogman flippers and 3-pronged harpoon gun.	BRITANNIA

PART II

Scene 6

Set onstage

Roughly made bench under hut window.
2 coconuts downstage of door opening.
Goatskin umbrella upstage of door.

Off R.

Spears.	CHORUS
Length of rope.	1 of CHORUS

Off L.

Knife and treasure island map.	ROBINSON
In hut - long muzzled gun, ramrod and rag.	ROBINSON

Scene 7

Off R.

Bag and treasure maps as in Scene 1 with one map drawn as a perfect square with an "X" in the middle in addition.	ROGER
Placard on stick reading, "JOLLY ROGER & RUEFUL RUPERT, HIRE SERVICE PIRATES".	ROGER
Placard on stick reading, "SAM SKUL-DUGGERY & CUTTHROAT CUTHBERT, HIRE SERVICE PIRATES".	1 of CHORUS
Placard on stick reading, "HIGH JACK & LOW JOHN, HIRE SERVICE PIRATES".	1 of CHORUS
Placard to be hung round neck reading, "GENUINE PIRATE TREASURE MAPS". Treasure maps of triangles with an "X" in the middle.	1 of CHORUS
Sandwich board reading, "MRS CRUSOE'S BOARDING HOUSE - 'MON CARIBBEAN REPOS' 3 ~~2~~ ~~1~~, FISH ROW, PORT OF SPAIN". (This needs to be made sufficiently strong to be a stretcher for BROODY.)	BILLY
Pencil.	BILLY

Scene 8

Set onstage

D.L. Table with three chairs round it.
Bowl covered by a towel on table.

Off R.

2 eye patches and false black moustache.	BILLY
Placard on stick reading, "BARNACLE BILL, HIRE SERVICE PIRATE".	BILLY
Large prop. thermometer.	WILL ATKINS.
False black moustache on an elastic.	SUKEY
Tankard.	SUKEY

2 Tankards.	POLLY & SUKEY

Off L.

Crutch with "L" plate to hang on it.	MRS CRUSOE
Tankard with 2 straws.	SERVING WENCH

Scene 9

Off R.

Battered old wooden treasure chest.	ROBINSON & FRIDAY
Spear.	FRIDAY
Small portable record player.	MRS CRUSOE
3 spears.	3 of CHORUS

Off L.

Huge gramophone record, with H.M.V. label on one side and the title, "HUSH-A-BYE-BABY". The Song Sheet words are printed on the reverse. (The record should be about 6 ft in diameter and about 4 ins thick in order to balance easily by itself. It requires a central spindle to revolve round.)	1 of CHORUS

Scene 10

Set onstage

Bench against L. side of central wall.

Off R.

Treasure chest (as in Scene 9). Golden goblet set inside chest.	ROBINSON
2 spears.	2 of CHORUS
Cannon ball, (black painted rubber ball).	To be thrown on.
Fine line.	To attach to WILL's hat.
2nd Cannon ball.	To be thrown on.
Prop. cannon, (the barrel is detachable and has paper pasted over the breech end so that the cannon ball can be pushed through).	ROGER & RUPERT
Ramrod.	ROGER
Small keg of gunpowder.	WILL ATKINS
Cutlasses.	CHORUS PIRATES

Mugs.	WILL & PIRATES
Off L.	
Prop. cannon, (breech end also has paper pasted over).	BILLY & SUKEY
Ramrod.	BILLY
Cannon ball.	MRS CRUSOE
Small keg of gunpowder.	MRS CRUSOE
Splayed out end to fit on cannon barrel.	ROGER & RUPERT
Dried peas.	To be blown through tubing as sunflower seeds.
In hut – 2 guns.	FRIDAY
Pair of pistols.	ROBINSON
Broom with white flag on end of handle and huge kettle.	MRS CRUSOE
Mugs.	ROBINSON & FRIDAY
Tray with large teapot and 5 mugs.	POLLY
In Flies	
Chicken.	To be thrown on.

Scene 11

Set onstage

Wheelstool, with downstage wheel disguised as a Union Jack emblazoned shield.
Fine line attached to stool going off R.
Champagne bottle on stool.

Off L.	
Prop. rose.	DAVY JONES

Scene 12

Off R.	
Bo'sun's pipe.	1 of CHORUS
Off L.	
Bo'sun's pipe.	1 of CHORUS

PART I

Scene 1

1.	Jingle of housebell.	Off R.
2.	Town clock chiming and striking 12.	Off as convenient

Scene 3

3.	Ship's bell sounding 6 bells.	Off as convenient
4.	Ship's bell sounding 7 bells.	Off as convenient
5.	Ship's bell sounding 8 bells.	Off as convenient
6.	Wind noise and thunder rolls, (wind continues into beginning of Scene 4).	Wind machine and tape, grams or thunder sheet

Part II

Scene 6

7.	Jungle bird song.	Tape or grams
8.	Gunshot.	Starter's pistol off L.
9.	Gunshot.	Starter's pistol off L.

Scene 7

10.	Long rumbling crash.	Off R., several buckets of broken glass, bricks to drop & boxes to bang: or tape

Scene 10

11.	Cannon shot.	Maroon off R.
12.	Cannon shot.	Maroon off R.
13.	Gunshot.	Starter's pistol off L.
14.	Cannon shot.	Maroon off R.
15.	Gunshot.	Starter's pistol off L.
16.	Loud crash.	Off L., a log thrown down forcefully & a glass crash (bucket of broken glass thrown into an empty bucket)
17.	Gunshot.	Starter's pistol off R.

PART I

1.	Overture.	Orchestra

Scene 1

2.	"HEAVE HO!", Opening Chorus	CHORUS
3.	BILLY's entrance music	Orchestra
4.	SUKEY's entrance music	Orchestra
5.	"MY DAY"	BILLY & SUKEY
6.	POLLY's entrance music, (Pretty Polly Perkins)	Orchestra
7.	"PRETTY"	POLLY
8.	MRS CRUSOE's entrance music	Orchestra
9.	"SOMETHING'S BOUND TO TURN UP"	MRS CRUSOE
10.	BRITANNIA's entrance music, (Rule Britannia)	Orchestra
11.	"ANY MOMENT NOW" Segue into	CHORUS
12.	"HOME AGAIN"	ROBINSON & CHORUS
13.	BROODY's entrance music	Orchestra
14.	"PRETTY POLLY"	ROBINSON & POLLY
15.	WILL ATKINS's entrance music	Orchestra
16.	PIRATE's entrance music, (A Life on the Ocean Wave)	Orchestra
17.	"HEAVE HO!" reprise. (Continue, orchestra only, as link to next scene and segue into cue 18.)	Ensemble

Scene 2

18.	"RULE BRITANNIA" reprise 10.	Orchestra
19.	Conspiratorial entrance music, reprise 15.	Orchestra
20.	"BLUES". (Continue, orchestra only, as link to next scene.)	WILL, ROGER & RUPERT

Scene 3

21.	"SAILORS' CHORES"	Ensemble
22.	"NEARBY"	ROBINSON & POLLY
23.	Conspiratorial entrance music, reprise 15.	Orchestra
24.	Fight music	Orchestra

25.	Shipwreck music, (continues into next scene. At end of U.V. sequence segue into cue 26.)	Orchestra

Scene 4

26.	"DOWN BELOW"	DAVY JONES

Scene 5

27.	Ballet	CHORUS
28.	Transformation and finale	Orchestra

29.	Entr'acte	Orchestra

PART II

Scene 6

30.	Dawn music	Orchestra
31.	"PRETTY POLLY", reprise 14.	ROBINSON & POLLY
32.	MAN FRIDAY's entrance music	Orchestra
33.	Cannibal Dance	Drums
34.	"THE WAY TO THE TOP" (Repeat, orchestra only, as link to next scene.)	FRIDAY & ROBINSON

Scene 7

35.	"IF I JUST CLOSE MY EYES"	POLLY

Scene 8

36.	Opening music, reprise 20, (fade to dialogue)	Orchestra
37.	Tango	Orchestra
38.	MRS CRUSOE's entrance music	Orchestra
39.	Tango, reprise 37 under dialogue	Orchestra
40.	"CALYPSO", (repeat, orchestra only, as link to next scene)	Ensemble

Scene 9

41.	"RAH! RAH! RAH!" Song sheet	MRS CRUSOE, FRIDAY & AUDIENCE
42.	Chase music, (continue as link to next scene)	Orchestra

Scene 10

43.	"POLLY PUT THE KETTLE ON"	Ensemble
44.	"RULE BRITANNIA", reprise 10	Orchestra
45.	"LET'S GO HOME NOW"	Ensemble
46.	"RULE BRITANNIA", reprise 10 for scene link and fade to dialogue in Scene 11	Orchestra

Scene 11

47.	"RULE BRITANNIA"	BRITANNIA & DAVY JONES

Scene 12

48.	"HEAVE HO!", reprise 2 for walk down	Orchestra
49.	"LET'S GO HOME NOW", reprise 45	Tutti